THE COMPLETE
WOMEN'S WORLD CUP
FOOTBALL
TOURNAMENTS
1991-2015

Dirk Karsdorp

British Library Cataloguing in Publication Data
A catalogue record for this book is available from the British Library

ISBN: 978-1-86223-372-0

Copyright © 2018, SOCCER BOOKS LIMITED (01472 696226)
72 St. Peter's Avenue, Cleethorpes, N.E. Lincolnshire, DN35 8HU, England
Web site   www.soccer-books.co.uk
e-mail   info@soccer-books.co.uk

Printed in the UK by 4edge Ltd.

AN INTRODUCTION TO
THE FIFA WOMEN'S WORLD CUP

Although the first World Cup for men was organised by FIFA in 1930, the creation of a similar competition for women wasn't considered for many years. This is not perhaps surprising in view of the attitude to women's football in many countries for much of the 20th Century. In the present, it is hard to believe that the English Football Association only lifted a 50-year ban on women's teams playing on their members' pitches as late as 1971!

Taking this into account, it is perhaps understandable that, although women's football had become very popular in many countries over the years, it wasn't until June 1988 that FIFA organised an invitational tournament in China as a test to see if a Women's World Cup competition would be viable. Twelve national teams took part in this invitational competition – four from UEFA, three from AFC, two from CONCACAF and one each from CONMEBOL, CAF and OFC. The matches were played between 1st and 12th June and, such was the success of the tournament, FIFA approved the establishment of an official Women's World Cup a little over two weeks later, on 30th June 1988! It was decided that the inaugural Women's World Cup was to take place in 1991, with China once again hosting the finals tournament. Twelve teams competed in the 1991 finals (following a qualification process which whittled down the 48 countries to enter the competition), and the United States beat Norway 2-1 in the Final to be crowned the first Women's World Champions. Since then, the scope of the competition has continued to grow with 16 teams competing in the 1999 finals tournament (with 67 countries in the qualifiers) and 24 finalists in 2015 (with 134 countries in the qualifiers).

This book covers the matches played in each of the seven Women's FIFA World Cup finals tournaments held between 1991 and 2015. Complete and comprehensive statistics are included for each of the 232 finals games played during this period.

A series of sister publications containing complete statistics for the men's

FIFA World Cup competitions from 1930 through to 2014 is also published by Soccer Books. These include all qualification matches in addition to the finals matches and a further book covering the 2018 FIFA World Cup will be published later in the year.

Details of all of our World Cup titles as well as many other statistical books can be found on the back cover of this publication.

FIFA WOMEN'S WORLD CUP – CHINA PR 1991

GROUP STAGE

GROUP A

16.11.1991 Tianhe Stadium, Guangzhou: China PR – Norway 4-0 (1-0)
China PR: ZHONG Honglian, WEN Lirong, NIU Lijie, MA Li, LIU Ailing, ZHOU Yang, ZHOU Hua, SUN Qingmei, LI Xiufu, SUN Wen (70' ZHU Tao), WU Weiying (47' SHUI Qingxia). (Coach: SHANG Ruihua).
Norway: Reidun SETH, Linda MEDALEN, Tina SVENSSON, Gro ESPESETH (62' Anette IGLAND), Agnete CARLSEN, Gunn Lisbeth NYBORG, Hege RIISE, Tone HAUGEN, Heidi STØRE, Catherine ZABOROWSKI, Birthe HEGSTAD (59' Ellen SCHEEL). (Coach: Even PELLERUD).
Goals: 22' MA Li 1-0, 45', 50' LIU Ailing 2-0, 3-0, 75' SUN Qingmei 4-0.
Referee: Salvador IMPERATORE MARCONE (Chile) Attendance: 65.000

17.11.1991 Tianhe Stadium, Guangzhou: Denmark – New Zealand 3-0 (2-0)
Denmark: Helle BJERREGAARD, Karina SEFRON, Jannie HANSEN, Bonny MADSEN, Lisbet KOLDING (64' Lotte BAGGE), Susan MACKENSIE, Irene STELLING, Marianne JENSEN, Helle JENSEN, Annie GAM-PEDERSEN, Hanne NISSEN (54' Annette THYCHOSEN). (Coach: Keld GANTZHORN).
New Zealand: Leslie Catherine KING Moore, Jocelyn Edna PARR, Cinnamon June CHANEY (41' Teresa Ann (Terry) McCAHILL), Kim Barbara NYE, Deborah Anne PULLEN Kok, Maureen Dale JACOBSON, Monique Annette VAN DE ELZEN, Donna Marie BAKER (54' Lorraine Robin TAYLOR), Julia Petryce CAMPBELL, Wendi Judith HENDERSON, Amanda Anne CRAWFORD. (Coach: Dave BOARDMAN).
Goals: 15', 40' Helle JENSEN 1-0, 2-0, 42' Susan MACKENSIE 3-0.
Referee: Omer YENGO (Congo) Attendance: 14.000

18.11.1991 Guangdong Provincial People's Stadium, Guangzhou:
        Norway – New Zealand 4-0 (3-0)
Norway: Reidun SETH, Linda MEDALEN (YC34), Tina SVENSSON, Agnete CARLSEN, Gunn Lisbeth NYBORG, Hege RIISE, Tone HAUGEN (76' Margunn HUMLESTØL Haugenes), Heidi STØRE, Catherine ZABOROWSKI, Liv STRÆDET, Birthe HEGSTAD (59' Ellen SCHEEL). (Coach: Even PELLERUD).
New Zealand: Leslie Catherine KING Moore, Cinnamon June CHANEY (28' Lynley Joy PEDRUCO Lucas), Kim Barbara NYE, Teresa Ann (Terry) McCAHILL, Deborah Anne PULLEN Kok, Lorraine Robin TAYLOR, Maureen Dale JACOBSON, Donna Marie BAKER, Julia Petryce CAMPBELL, Wendi Judith HENDERSON, Amanda Anne CRAWFORD (45' Monique Annette VAN DE ELZEN). (Coach: Dave BOARDMAN).
Goals: 30' Teresa Ann (Terry) McCAHILL 1-0 (og), 32', 38' Linda MEDALEN 2-0, 3-0, 49' Hege RIISE 4-0.
Referee: Salvador Imperatore MARCONE (Chile) Attendance: 12.000

5

19.11.1991 Guangdong Provincial People's Stadium, Guangzhou:
China PR – Denmark   2-2 (1-1)
China PR: ZHONG Honglian, WEN Lirong, NIU Lijie (71' WEI Haiying), MA Li, LIU
Ailing, ZHOU Yang, ZHOU Hua, SUN Qingmei, LI Xiufu (YC50), SUN Wen, WU Weiying
(59' ZHANG Yan). (Coach: SHANG Ruihua).
Denmark: Helle BJERREGAARD, Karina SEFRON, Jannie HANSEN, Bonny MADSEN,
Mette NIELSEN, Lisbet KOLDING, Susan MACKENSIE, Irene STELLING, Helle JENSEN,
Annie GAM-PEDERSEN, Hanne NISSEN (71' Lotte BAGGE). (Coach: Keld
GANTZHORN).
Goals: 24' Lisbet KOLDING 0-1, 37' SUN Wen 1-1, 55' Hanne NISSEN 1-2,
76' WEI Haiying 2-2.
Referee: Vassilios NIKKAKIS (Greece) Attendance: 27.000

21.11.1991 New Plaza Stadium, Foshan: China PR – New Zealand 4-1 (3-0)
China PR: ZHONG Honglian, WEN Lirong, NIU Lijie, MA Li, LIU Ailing, ZHOU Yang,
ZHOU Hua, SUN Qingmei, LI Xiufu (28' SHUI Qingxia), SUN Wen, WU Weiying (63' WEI
Haiying). (Coach: SHANG Ruihua).
New Zealand: Leslie Catherine KING Moore, Lynley Joy PEDRUCO Lucas, Kim Barbara
NYE, Teresa Ann (Terry) McCAHILL, Deborah Anne PULLEN Kok, Lorraine Robin
TAYLOR, Maureen Dale JACOBSON, Monique Annette VAN DE ELZEN, Donna Marie
BAKER (26' Amanda Anne CRAWFORD), Lynne WARRING (65' Julia Petryce
CAMPBELL), Wendi Judith HENDERSON. (Coach: Dave BOARDMAN).
Goals: 20' ZHOU Yang 1-0, 22' LIU Ailing 2-0, 24' WU Weiying 3-0, 60' LIU Ailing 4-0,
65' Kim Barbara NYE 4-1.
Referee: Gyanu Raja SHRESTA (Nepal) Attendance: 14.000

21.11.1991 Ying Dong Stadium, Panyu: Norway – Denmark 2-1 (1-0)
Norway: Reidun SETH, Linda MEDALEN (YC30) (62' Ellen SCHEEL), Tina SVENSSON,
Agnete CARLSEN, Gunn Lisbeth NYBORG (YC33), Hege RIISE, Tone HAUGEN, Heidi
STØRE, Catherine ZABOROWSKI, Liv STRÆDET (29' Gro ESPESETH), Birthe
HEGSTAD. (Coach: Even PELLERUD).
Denmark: Helle BJERREGAARD, Karina SEFRON, Jannie HANSEN, Bonny MADSEN,
Mette NIELSEN (41' Annette THYCHOSEN), Lisbet KOLDING, Susan MACKENSIE, Irene
STELLING, Helle JENSEN, Annie GAM-PEDERSEN, Hanne NISSEN (50' Marianne
JENSEN). (Coach: Keld GANTZHORN).
Goals: 14' Tina SVENSSON 1-0 (p), 54' Annette THYCHOSEN 1-1 (p),
56' Linda MEDALEN 2-1.
Referee: Vadim ZHUK (USSR) Attendance: 15.500

Team	Pld	W	D	L	GF	GA	GD	Pts
China PR	3	2	1	0	10	3	7	5
Norway	3	2	0	1	6	5	1	4
Denmark	3	1	1	1	6	4	2	3
New Zealand	3	0	0	3	1	11	-10	0

GROUP B

17.11.1991 New Plaza Stadium, Foshan: Japan – Brazil 0-1 (0-1)
Japan: Masae SUZUKI, Midori HONDA, Mayumi KAJI, Sayuri YAMAGUCHI, Kyoko
KURODA, Asako Takemoto TAKAKURA (52' Yuriko MIZUMA), Futaba KIOKA, Kaori
NAGAMINE, Michiko MATSUDA, Akemi NODA, Takako TEZUKA. (Coach: Tamotsu
SUZUKI).
Brazil: Margarete Maria Pioresan "MEG", ELANE dos Santos Rêgo *(YC67)*, Rosilane
Camargo Mota "FANTA", MARISA Pires Nogueira (15' DORALICE Santos), SOLANGE
Santos Bastos, Maria Gomes de "ROSA" LIMA, MÁRCIA Honório da SILVA,
ROSÂNGELA ROCHA *(YC79)*, MARIA Lúcia da Silva LIMA *(YC58)*, ROSELI de Belo,
ADRIANA "VIOLA" Burke (70' CENIRA Sampaio Pereira do Prado). (Coach: FERNANDO
Luís Brederodes PIRES).
Goal: 4' ELANE Rego dos Santos 0-1.
Referee: LU Jun (China PR) Attendance: 14.000

17.11.1991 Ying Dong Stadium, Panyu: Sweden – United States 2-3 (0-1)
Sweden: Elisabeth LEIDINGE, Malin LUNDGREN, Anette HANSSON, Camilla FORS (54'
Ingrid JOHANSSON), Lena VIDEKULL, Eva ZEIKFALVY, Malin SWEDBERG, Marie
KARLSSON (64' Helen NILSSON), Pia Mariane SUNDHAGE, Anneli ANDELÉN, Helen
JOHANSSON *(YC64)*. (Coach: Gunilla PAIJKULL).
United States: Mary HARVEY, Joy Lynn FAWCETT Biefeld, Carla Werden OVERBECK,
Debbie Belkin RADEMACHER, Kristine Marie LILLY Heavey (33' Linda HAMILTON),
Julie Maurine FOUDY, Michelle Anne AKERS Stahl, Shannon Danise HIGGINS Cirovski,
Mariel Margaret (Mia) HAMM *(YC24)*, Carin JENNINGS Gabarra, April HEINRICHS.
(Coach: Anson DORRANCE).
Goals: 40', 49' Carin JENNINGS Gabarra 0-1, 0-2, 62' Mariel Margaret (Mia) HAMM 0-3,
65' Lena VIDEKULL 1-3, 71' Ingrid JOHANSSON 2-3.
Referee: John TORO RENDÓN (Colombia) Attendance: 14.000

19.11.1991 New Plaza Stadium, Foshan: Japan – Sweden 0-8 (0-6)
Japan: Masae SUZUKI, Midori HONDA, Mayumi KAJI, Sayuri YAMAGUCHI *(YC55)*,
Kyoto KURODA, Asako Takemoto TAKAKURA, Futaba KIOKA, Kaori NAGAMINE (67'
Yuriko MIZUMA), Michiko MATSUDA, Akemi NODA, Takako TEZUKA. (Coach: Tamotsu
SUZUKI).
Sweden: Elisabeth LEIDINGE, Malin LUNDGREN, Anette HANSSON, Lena VIDEKULL
(41' Susanne HEDBERG), Eva ZEIKFALVY, Ingrid JOHANSSON, Marie KARLSSON, Pia
Mariane SUNDHAGE, Anneli ANDELÉN, Helen NILSSON, Helen JOHANSSON (35'
Camilla SVENSSON Gustafsson). (Coach: Gunilla PAIJKULL).
Goals: 1', 11' Lena VIDEKULL 0-1, 0-2, 15' Anneli ANDELÉN 0-3,
25' Malin LUNDGREN 0-4, 27' Helen NILSSON 0-5, 35' Pia Mariane SUNDHAGE 0-6,
60' Anneli ANDELÉN 0-7, 70' Sayuri YAMAGUCHI 0-7 (og).
Referee: Gyanu Raja SHRESTA (Nepal) Attendance: 14.000

7

19.11.1991 Ying Dong Stadium, Panyu: Brazil – United States 0-5 (0-4)
Brazil: Margarete Maria Pioresan "MEG", ELANE dos Santos Rêgo, Rosilane Camargo Mota "FANTA", MARISA Pires Nogueira, SOLANGE Santos Bastos (39' DORALICE Santos), Maria Gomes de "ROSA" LIMA, CENIRA Sampaio Pereira do Prado, MÁRCIA Honório da SILVA, MARILZA Martins da SILVA (46' Delma Gonçalves "PRETINHA"), ROSELI de Belo (YC70), Lunalva Torres de Almeida "NALVINHA". (Coach: FERNANDO Luís Brederodes PIRES).
United States: Mary HARVEY, Joy Lynn FAWCETT Biefeld, Carla Werden OVERBECK, Linda HAMILTON, Kristine Marie LILLY Heavey (67' Debbie Belkin RADEMACHER), Julie Maurine FOUDY, Michelle Anne AKERS Stahl, Shannon Danise HIGGINS Cirovski, Mariel Margaret (Mia) HAMM, Carin JENNINGS Gabarra, April HEINRICHS (41' Brandi Denise CHASTAIN). (Coach: Anson DORRANCE).
Goals: 23', 35' April HEINRICHS 0-1, 0-2, 38' Carin JENNINGS Gabarra 0-3, 39' Michelle Anne AKERS Stahl 0-4, 63' Mariel Margaret (Mia) HAMM 0-5.
Referee: Vadim ZHUK (Belarus) Attendance: 15.500

21.11.1991 New Plaza Stadium, Foshan: Japan – United States 0-3 (0-3)
Japan: Masae SUZUKI, Midori HONDA, Mayumi KAJI, Sayuri YAMAGUCHI, Kyoto KURODA, Asako Takemoto TAKAKURA (60' Etsuko HANDA), Futaba KIOKA, Kaori NAGAMINE, Michiko MATSUDA, Akemi NODA, Takako TEZUKA. (Coach: Tamotsu SUZUKI).
United States: Mary HARVEY, Carla Werden OVERBECK (YC31), Linda HAMILTON, Lori Ann HENRY, Debbie Belkin RADEMACHER, Brandi Denise CHASTAIN, Julie Maurine FOUDY, Michelle Anne AKERS Stahl (41' Mariel Margaret (Mia) HAMM), Tracey LEONE Bates, Carin JENNINGS Gabarra (41' Kristine Marie LILLY Heavey), Wendy GEBAUER Palladino. (Coach: Anson DORRANCE).
Goals: 20', 37' Michelle Anne AKERS Stahl 0-1, 0-2, 39' Wendy GEBAUER Palladino 0-3.
Referee: John Jairo TORO RENDÓN (Colombia) Attendance: 14.000

21.11.1991 Ying Dong Stadium, Panyu: Brazil – Sweden 0-2 (0-1)
Brazil: Margarete Maria Pioresan "MEG", ELANE dos Santos Rêgo, Rosilane Camargo Mota "FANTA", MARISA Pires Nogueira, Maria Gomes de "ROSA" LIMA, DORALICE Santos, CENIRA Sampaio Pereira do Prado, MÁRCIA TAFFAREL, MÁRCIA Honório da SILVA (60' Delma Gonçalves "PRETINHA"), ROSELI de Belo, ADRIANA "VIOLA" Burke (62' Lunalva Torres de Almeida "NALVINHA"). (Coach: FERNANDO Luís Brederodes PIRES).
Sweden: Ing-Marie OLSSON, Camila FORS, Marie EWRELIUS, Camilla SVENSSON Gustafsson, Susanne HEDBERG, Malin SWEDBERG, Marie KARLSSON (41' Ingrid JOHANSSON), Pernilla LARSSON, Pia Mariane SUNDHAGE, Anneli ANDELÉN, Helen NILSSON. (Coach: Gunilla PAIJKULL).
Goals: 42' Pia Mariane SUNDHAGE 0-1 (p), 56' Susanne HEDBERG 0-2.
Referee: LU Jun (China PR) Attendance: 12.000

8

Team	Pld	W	D	L	GF	GA	GD	Pts
United States	*3*	*3*	*0*	*0*	*11*	*2*	*9*	*6*
Sweden	*3*	*2*	*0*	*1*	*12*	*3*	*9*	*4*
Brazil	3	1	0	2	1	7	-6	2
Japan	3	0	0	3	0	12	-12	0

GROUP C

17.11.1991 Jiangmen Stadium, Jiangmen: Germany – Nigeria 4-0 (3-0)
Germany: Marion ISBERT, Doris FITSCHEN, Birgitt AUSTERMÜHL, Jutta
NARDENBACH, Silvia NEID (36' Roswitha BINDL), Martina VOSS-TECKLENBURG,
Bettina WIEGMANN, Britta UNSLEBER (35' Frauke KUHLMANN), Petra DAMM, Heidi
MOHR, Gudrun GOTTSCHLICH. (Coach: Gero BISANZ).
Nigeria: Ann CHIEJINE, Florence OMAGBEMI, Mavis OGUN, Omo-Love BRANCH,
Phoebe EBIMIEKUMO, Diana NWAIWU, Nkiru OKOSIEME, Ann MUKORO, Ngozi
UCHE (41' Chioma AJUNWA), Rita NWADIKE, Adaku OKOROAFOR (34' Gift
SHOWEMIMO). (Coach: Johannes (Jo) BONFRERE).
Goals: 16' Silvia NEID 1-0, 32', 34' Heidi MOHR 2-0, 3-0, 57' Gudrun GOTTSCHLICH 4-0.
Referee: Rafael RODRÍGUEZ Medina (El Salvador) Attendance: 14.000

17.11.1991 Jiangmen Stadium, Jiangmen: Chinese Taipei – Italy 0-5 (0-3)
Chinese Taipei: HONG Li-Chyn, CHEN Shwu Ju, LO Chu-Yin, HSU Chia Cheng, LAN Lan
Fen, CHOU Tai Ying, SHIEH Su Jean, WU Su-Ching, LIN Mei Jih (49' WU Min Hsun),
HUANG Yu Chuan (62' LIN Mei Chun), KO Chiao Lin. (Coach: CHING Tsu-Pin).
Italy: Stefania ANTONINI, Marina CORDENONS, Rafaella SAIMASO, Muara FURLOTTI
(48' Emma IOZZELLI), Maria MARIOTTI, Federica D'ASTOLFO, Feriana FERRAGUZZI,
Adele MARSILETTI, Fabiana CORRERA (59' Nausica PEDERSOLI), Silvia FIORINI
(YC59), Carolina MORACE. (Coach: Sergio GUENZA).
Goals: 15' Feriana FERRAGUZZI 0-1, 29' Adele MARSILETTI 0-2,
37', 52', 66' Carolina MORACE 0-3, 0-4, 0-5.
Referee: Fathi BOUCETTA (Tunisia) Attendance: 11.000

9

19.11.1991 Zhongshan Sports Center Stadium, Zhongshan: Italy – Nigeria 1-0 (0-0)
Italy: Stefania ANTONINI, Paola BONATO (63' Anna Maria MEGA), Marina
CORDENONS, Muara FURLOTTI, Elisabeth BAVAGNOLI (36' Maria MARIOTTI),
Federica D'ASTOLFO, Feriana FERRAGUZZI, Adele MARSILETTI, Fabiana CORRERA,
Silvia FIORINI, Carolina MORACE. (Coach: Sergio GUENZA).
Nigeria: Ann CHIEJINE, Florence OMAGBEMI, Mavis OGUN, Ngozi EZEOCHA, Omo-
Love BRANCH, Diana NWAIWU (78' Nkechi MBILITAM), Edith ELUMA *(YC75)*, Nkiru
OKOSIEME, Ngozi UCHE (73' Rachael YAMALA), Rita NWADIKE, Chioma AJUNWA.
(Coach: Johannes (Jo) BONFRERE).
Goal: 68' Carolina MORACE 1-0.
Referee: James McCLUSKEY (Scotland) Attendance: 12.000

19.11.1991 Zhongshan Sports Center Stadium, Zhongshan:
            Chinese Taipei – Germany 0-3 (0-2)
Chinese Taipei: LIN Hui Fang, CHEN Shwu Ju, LO Chu-Yin, HSU Chia Cheng, LAN Lan
Fen, WU Min Hsun, CHOU Tai Ying, SHIEH Su Jean, WU Su-Ching, HUANG Yu Chuan
(66' LIU Hsiu Mei), KO Chiao Lin (46' LIN Mei Chun). (Coach: CHING Tsu-Pin).
Germany: Marion ISBERT, Doris FITSCHEN, Birgitt AUSTERMÜHL (61' Beate WENDT),
Jutta NARDENBACH (41' Frauke KUHLMANN), Christine PAUL, Martina VOSS-
TECKLENBURG, Bettina WIEGMANN, Roswitha BINDL, Petra DAMM, Heidi MOHR,
Gudrun GOTTSCHLICH. (Coach: Gero BISANZ).
Goals: 10' Bettina WIEGMANN 0-1 (p), 21', 50' Heidi MOHR 0-2, 0-3.
Referee: Fathi BOUCETTA (Tunisia) Attendance: 10.000

21.11.1991 Jiangmen Stadium, Jiangmen: Chinese Taipei – Nigeria 2-0 (1-0)
Chinese Taipei: LIN Hui Fang, CHEN Shwu Ju, LO Chu-Yin, HSU Chia Cheng, LAN Lan
Fen, WU Min Hsun, LIU Hsiu Mei (6' HONG Li-Chyn *goalkeeper*), CHOU Tai Ying, SHIEH
Su Jean, WU Su-Ching (78' LIN Mei Jih), LIN Mei Chun. (Coach: CHING Tsu-Pin).
Nigeria: Ann CHIEJINE, Florence OMAGBEMI (60' Ann MUKORO), Mavis OGUN, Ngozi
EZEOCHA (41' Rachael YAMALA), Omo-Love BRANCH, Diana NWAIWU, Edith
ELUMA, Nkiru OKOSIEME, Ngozi UCHE *(YC46)*, Rita NWADIKE, Chioma AJUNWA.
(Coach: Johannes (Jo) BONFRERE).
Goals: 38' LIN Mei Chun 1-0, 55' CHOU Tai Ying 2-0.
Referee: Rafael RODRIGUEZ Medina (El Salvador) Attendance: 14.000

Sent-off: 6' LIN Hui Fang.

21.11.1991 Zhongshan Sports Center Stadium, Zhongshan:
Italy – Germany 0-2 (0-0)
Italy: Stefania ANTONINI, Marina CORDENONS, Rafaella SAIMASO, Emma IOZZELLI,
Elisabeth BAVAGNOLI, Maria MARIOTTI, Federica D'ASTOLFO, Feriana FERRAGUZZI
(YC50), Adele MARSILETTI, Silvia FIORINI (34' Anna Maria MEGA, 64' Fabiana
CORRERA), Carolina MORACE. (Coach: Sergio GUENZA).
Germany: Marion ISBERT, Doris FITSCHEN, Birgitt AUSTERMÜHL, Christine PAUL,
Martina VOSS-TECKLENBURG, Bettina WIEGMANN, Britta UNSLEBER *(YC50)*,
Roswitha BINDL, Sandra HENGST (41' Frauke KUHLMANN), Heidi MOHR, Gudrun
GOTTSCHLICH (68' Beate WENDT). (Coach: Gero BISANZ).
Goals: 67' Heidi MOHR 0-1, 79' Britta UNSLEBER 0-2.
Referee: James McCluskey (Scotland) Attendance: 12.000

Team	Pld	W	D	L	GF	GA	GD	Pts
Germany	3	3	0	0	9	0	9	6
Italy	3	2	0	1	6	2	4	4
Chinese Taipei	3	1	0	2	2	8	-6	2
Nigeria	3	0	0	3	0	7	-7	0

QUARTER-FINALS

24.11.1991 Zhongshan Sports Center Stadium, Zhongshan:
Denmark – Germany 1-2 (1-1, 1-1)
Denmark: Helle BJERREGAARD, Karina SEFRON *(YC17)*, Bonny MADSEN, Mette
NIELSEN, Lisbet KOLDING, Susan MACKENSIE, Irene STELLING, Helle JENSEN (73'
Janne RASMUSSEN), Annie GAM-PEDERSEN *(YC70)*, Hanne NISSEN (47' Lotte
BAGGE), Annette THYCHOSEN. (Coach: Keld GANTZHORN).
Germany: Marion ISBERT, Doris FITSCHEN, Birgitt AUSTERMÜHL *(YC37)*, Frauke
KUHLMANN, Christine PAUL, Martina VOSS-TECKLENBURG, Bettina WIEGMANN,
Roswitha BINDL (89' Beate WENDT), Petra DAMM, Heidi MOHR, Gudrun
GOTTSCHLICH (51' Britta UNSLEBER). (Coach: Gero BISANZ).
Goals: 17' Bettina WIEGMANN 0-1 (p), 25' Susan MACKENSIE 1-1 (p),
98' Heidi MOHR 1-2.
Referee: Vassilios NIKAKIS (Greece) Attendance: 12.000

Germany qualified after extra time.

24.11.1991 Tianhe Stadium, Guangzhou: China PR – Sweden 0-1 (0-1)
China PR: ZHONG Honglian, WEN Lirong, MA Li *(YC66)*, LIU Ailing, ZHOU Yang, ZHOU
Hua, SUN Qingmei, LI Xiufu, SUN Wen, WU Weiying (75' NIU Lijie), ZHANG Yan (46'
WEI Haiying). (Coach: SHANG Ruihua).
Sweden: Elisabeth LEIDINGE, Malin LUNDGREN *(YC39)*, Anette HANSSON, Lena
VIDEKULL, Eva ZEIKFALVY, Ingrid JOHANSSON, Marie KARLSSON, Pia Mariane
SUNDHAGE, Anneli ANDELÉN *(YC58)*, Helen NILSSON (67' Susanne HEDBERG), Helen
JOHANSSON *(YC57)* (65' Marie EWRELIUS). (Coach: Gunilla PAIJKULL).
Goal: 3' Pia Mariane SUNDHAGE 0-1.
Referee: John Jairo TORO Rendón (Colombia)   Attendance: 55.000

24.11.1991 Jiangmen Stadium, Jiangmen: Norway – Italy 3-2 (1-1, 2-2)
Norway: Reidun SETH, Tina SVENSSON, Agnete CARLSEN, Gunn Lisbeth NYBORG,
Margunn Humlestøl HAUGENES (79' Anette IGLAND), Hege RIISE *(YC37)*, Tone
HAUGEN, Heidi STØRE, Catherine ZABOROWSKI, Birthe HEGSTAD, Ellen SCHEEL.
(Coach: Even PELLERUD).
Italy: Stefania ANTONINI, Marina CORDENONS *(YC20)*, Rafaella SAIMASO (36' Paola
BONATO), Emma IOZZELLI, Elisabeth BAVAGNOLI, Maria MARIOTTI (68' Rita
GUARINO), Federica D'ASTOLFO, Feriana FERRAGUZZI, Adele MARSILETTI, Silvia
FIORINI, Carolina MORACE. (Coach: Sergio GUENZA).
Goals: 22' Birthe HEGSTAD 1-0, 31' Rafaella SAIMASO 1-1, 67' Agnete CARLSEN 2-1,
80' Rita GUARINO 2-2, 96' Tina SVENSSON 3-2 (p).
Referee: Rafael RODRIGUEZ Medina (El Salvador)   Attendance: 13.000

Norway qualified after extra time.

24.11.1991 New Plaza Stadium, Foshan: United States – Chinese Taipei 7-0 (4-0)
United States: Mary HARVEY, Joy Lynn FAWCETT Biefeld, Carla Werden OVERBECK
(57' Lori Ann HENRY), Linda HAMILTON, Kristine Marie LILLY Heavey, Julie Maurine
FOUDY, Michelle Anne AKERS Stahl, Shannon Danise HIGGINS Cirovski, Mariel Margaret
(Mia) HAMM), Carin JENNINGS Gabarra, April HEINRICHS (41' Debbie Belkin
RADEMACHER). (Coach: Anson DORRANCE).
Chinese Taipei: HONG Li-Chyn, CHEN Shwu Ju *(YC23)*, LO Chu-Yin, HSU Chia Cheng,
LAN Lan Fen, WU Min Hsun, CHOU Tai Ying, SHIEH Su Jean, WU Su-Ching (74' LIU Hsiu
Mei), CHEN Shu Chin, LIN Mei Chun. (Coach: CHING Tsu-Pin).
Goals: 8', 29', 33' Michelle Anne AKERS Stahl 1-0, 2-0, 3-0, 38' Julie Maurine FOUDY 4-0,
44', 48' Michelle Anne AKERS Stahl 5-0 (p), 6-0, 79' Joy Lynn FAWCETT Biefeld 7-0.
Referee: Omer YENGO (Congo)   Attendance: 12.000

12

SEMI-FINALS

27.11.1991   Ying Dong Stadium, Guanghzhou: Sweden – Norway 1-4 (1-1)
Sweden: Elisabeth LEIDINGE, Malin LUNDGREN, Anette HANSSON (51' Helen
NILSSON), Marie EWRELIUS, Lena VIDEKULL, Susanne HEDBERG (63' Malin
SWEDBERG), Eva ZEIKFALVY, Ingrid JOHANSSON, Marie KARLSSON, Pia Mariane
SUNDHAGE, Anneli ANDELÉN. (Coach: Gunilla PAIJKULL).
Norway: Reidun SETH, Linda MEDALEN, Tina SVENSSON (61' Anette IGLAND), Gro
ESPESETH, Agnete CARLSEN, Gunn Lisbeth NYBORG, Hege RIISE, Tone HAUGEN,
Heidi STØRE, Catherine ZABOROWSKI, Birthe HEGSTAD. (Coach: Even PELLERUD).
Goals: 6' Lena VIDEKULL 1-0, 39' Tina SVENSSON 1-1 (p), 41' Linda MEDALEN 1-2,
67' Agnete CARLSEN 1-3, 77' Linda MEDALEN 1-4.
Referee: James McCLUSKEY (Scotland)   Attendance: 16.000

27.11.1991   Guangdong Provincial People's Stadium, Guangzhou:
            Germany – United States 2-5 (1-3)
Germany: Marion ISBERT, Doris FITSCHEN *(YC59)*, Birgitt AUSTERMÜHL (60' Britta
UNSLEBER), Jutta NARDENBACH, Frauke KUHLMANN, Christine PAUL, Martina
VOSS-TECKLENBURG, Bettina WIEGMANN, Roswitha BINDL, Heidi MOHR, Gudrun
GOTTSCHLICH (50' Beate WENDT). (Coach: Gero BISANZ).
United States: Mary HARVEY, Joy Lynn FAWCETT Biefeld, Carla Werden OVERBECK,
Linda HAMILTON, Kristine Marie LILLY Heavey, Julie Maurine FOUDY, Michelle Anne
AKERS Stahl *(YC67)*, Shannon Danise HIGGINS Cirovski, Mariel Margaret (Mia) HAMM),
Carin JENNINGS Gabarra, April HEINRICHS. (Coach: Anson DORRANCE).
Goals: 10', 22', 33' Carin JENNINGS Gabarra 0-1, 0-2, 0-3, 34' Heidi MOHR 1-3,
54' April HEINRICHS 1-4, 63' Bettina WIEGMANN 2-4, 75' April HEINRICHS 2-5.
Referee: Salvador IMPERATORE Marcone (Chile)   Attendance: 15.000

THIRD PLACE MATCH

29.11.1991   Guangdong Provincial People's Stadium, Guangdong:
            Sweden – Germany 4-0 (4-0)
Sweden: Elisabeth LEIDINGE, Malin LUNDGREN, Marie EWRELIUS, Lena VIDEKULL,
Eva ZEIKFALVY, Malin SWEDBERG, Marie KARLSSON, Pia Mariane SUNDHAGE,
Anneli ANDELÉN *(YC60)*, Helen NILSSON *(YC53)*, Ingrid JOHANSSON. (Coach: Gunilla
PAIJKULL).
Germany: Marion ISBERT (38' Michaela KUBAT), Doris FITSCHEN, Jutta
NARDENBACH, Martina VOSS-TECKLENBURG, Bettina WIEGMANN, Britta
UNSLEBER, Roswitha BINDL (60' Elke WALTHER), Petra DAMM, Heidi MOHR, Beate
WENDT, Gudrun GOTTSCHLICH. (Coach: Gero BISANZ).
Goals: 7' Anneli ANDELÉN 1-0, 11' Pia Mariane SUNDHAGE 2-0,
29' Lena VIDEKULL 3-0, 43' Helen NILSSON 4-0.
Referee: CLAUDIA VASCONCELOS Guedes (Brazil)   Attendance: 20.000

FINAL

30.11.1991   Tianhe Stadium, Guangzhou: Norway – United States 1-2 (1-1)
Norway: Reidun SETH, Linda MEDALEN, Tina SVENSSON, Gro ESPESETH, Agnete
CARLSEN, Gunn Lisbeth NYBORG, Hege RIISE, Tone HAUGEN, Heidi STØRE, Catherine
ZABOROWSKI (79' Liv STRÆDET), Birthe HEGSTAD. (Coach: Even PELLERUD).
United States: Mary HARVEY, Joy Lynn FAWCETT Biefeld, Carla Werden OVERBECK,
Linda HAMILTON, Kristine Marie LILLY Heavey, Julie Maurine FOUDY, Michelle Anne
AKERS Stahl *(YC54)*, Shannon Danise HIGGINS Cirovski, Mariel Margaret (Mia) HAMM),
Carin JENNINGS Gabarra, April HEINRICHS. (Coach: Anson DORRANCE).
Goals: 20' Michelle Anne AKERS Stahl 0-1, 29' Linda MEDALEN 1-1,
78' Michelle Anne AKERS Stahl 1-2.
Referee: Vadim ZHUK (Belarus)   Attendance: 63.000

The United States won the first Women's World Cup.

FIFA WOMEN'S WORLD CUP – SWEDEN 1995

GROUP STAGE

GROUP A

05.06.1995 Tingvalla IP, Karlstad: Germany – Japan 1-0 (1-0)
Germany: Manuela GOLLER, Anouschka BERNHARD, Birgitt AUSTERMÜHL, Ursula LOHN, Silva NEID, Maren MEINERT, Martina VOSS-TECKLENBURG (65' Birgit PRINZ), Bettina WIEGMANN, Dagmar POHLMANN, Heidi MOHR, Patricia BROCKER Grigoli (82' Melanie HOFFMANN). (Coach: Gero BISANZ).
Japan: Junko OZAWA, Yumi OBE, Rie YAMAKI, Kae NISHINA, Yumi TOMEI, Maki HANETA, Homare SAWA, Asako Takemoto TAKAKURA, Futaba KIOKA (80' Etsuko HANDA), Tamaki UCHIYAMA (73' Kaori NAGAMINE), Akemi NODA. (Coach: Tamotsu SUZUKI).
Goal: 23' Silva NEID 1-0.
Referee: Petros MATHABELA (South Africa)   Attendance: 3.824

05.06.1995 Olympia, Helsingborg: Sweden – Brazil 0-1 (0-1)
Sweden: Elisabeth LEIDINGE *(YC75)*, Gärd Kristin BENTSSON, Malin LUNDGREN (43' Anna POHJANEN), Åsa JAKOBSSON (83' Sofia JOHANSSON), Malin Elisabeth ANDERSSON, Lena VIDEKULL, Anneli OLSSON (61' Susanne HEDBERG), Eva ZEIKFALVY, Pia Mariane SUNDHAGE, Anneli ANDELÉN, Ulrika KALTE. (Coach: Bengt SIMONSSON).
Brazil: Margarete Maria Pioresan "MEG", ELANE dos Santos Rêgo, Rosilane Camargo Mota "FANTA", SUZY Bitencourt de Oliveira, Sisleide do Amor Lima "SISSI", VALERIA Aparecida Bonifacio, LEDA MARIA Cozer Abreu (16' SOLANGE Santos Bastos, 83' TÂNIA Maria Pereira Ribeiro), CENIRA Sampaio do Prado, Delma Gonçalves "PRETINHA" *(YC21)*, Mariléia dos Santos "MICHAEL JACKSON" *(YC57)*, ROSELI de Belo. (Coach: ADEMAR FONSECA Júnior).
Goal: 37' ROSELI de Belo 0-1.
Referee: Sonia DENONCOURT (Canada)   Attendance: 14.500

07.06.1995 Olympia, Helsingborg: Sweden – Germany 3-2 (0-2)
Sweden: Elisabeth LEIDINGE, Gärd Kristin BENGTSSON (35' Åsa LÖNNQVIST), Åsa JAKOBSSON, Malin Elisabeth ANDERSSON, Anna POHJANEN (51' Malin FLINK), Lena VIDEKULL, Eva ZEIKFALVY (84' Anneli OLSSON), Pia Mariane SUNDHAGE, Anneli ANDELÉN, Ulrika KALTE, Helen NILSSON. (Coach: Bengt SIMONSSON).
Germany: Manuela GOLLER, Anouschka BERNHARD, Birgitt AUSTERMÜHL *(YC61)*, Ursula LOHN, Silva NEID *(YC14)*, Maren MEINERT, Martina VOSS-TECKLENBURG (84' Sandra MINNERT), Bettina WIEGMANN, Dagmar POHLMANN, Heidi MOHR, Patricia BROCKER Grigoli (57' Birgit PRINZ). (Coach: Gero BISANZ).
Goals: 9' Bettina WIEGMANN 0-1 (p), 42' Ursula LOHN 0-2,
65' Malin Elisabeth ANDERSSON 1-2 (p), 80' Pia Mariane SUNDHAGE 2-2,
86' Malin Elisabeth ANDERSSON 3-2.
Referee: Linda May BLACK (New Zealand)   Attendance: 5.855

07.06.1995 Tingvalla IP, Karlstad: Brazil – Japan 1-2 (1-2)
Brazil: Margarete Maria Pioresan "MEG", ELANE dos Santos Rêgo *(YC26)*, Rosilane
Camargo Mota "FANTA", SOLANGE Santos Bastos (72' Miraildes Maciel Mota
"FORMIGA"), SUZY Bitencourt de Oliveira, Sisleide do Amor Lima "SISSI", VALERIA
Aparecida Bonifacio, CENIRA Sampaio do Prado, Delma Gonçalves "PRETINHA", Mariléia
dos Santos "MICHAEL JACKSON" *(YC10)* (83' Lunalva Torres de Almeida "NALVINHA"),
ROSELI de Belo. (Coach: ADEMAR FONSECA Júnior).
Japan: Junko OZAWA, Yumi OBE *(YC48)*, Rie YAMAKI, Kae NISHINA, Maki HANETA,
Homare SAWA, Asako Takemoto TAKAKURA, Futaba KIOKA, Tamaki UCHIYAMA,
Nami OTAKE, Akemi NODA. (Coach: Tamotsu SUZUKI).
Goals: 7' Delma Gonçalves "PRETINHA" 1-0, 13', 45' Akemi NODA 1-1, 1-2.
Referee: Catherine Leann HEPBURN (United States) Attendance: 2.286

09.06.1995 Arosvallen, Västerås: Sweden – Japan 2-0 (0-0)
Sweden: Elisabeth LEIDINGE, Gärd Kristin BENGTSSON, Åsa JAKOBSSON (46' Anneli
OLSSON), Malin Elisabeth ANDERSSON, Anna POHJANEN (90' Malin FLINK), Lena
VIDEKULL, Eva ZEIKFALVY (58' Åsa LÖNNQVIST), Pia Mariane SUNDHAGE, Anneli
ANDELÉN, Ulrika KALTE, Helen NILSSON. (Coach: Bengt SIMONSSON).
Japan: Junko OZAWA, Yumi OBE, Rie YAMAKI *(YC15)*, Kae NISHINA, Maki HANETA,
Homare SAWA (76' Etsuko HANDA), Asako Takemoto TAKAKURA, Futaba KIOKA,
Tamaki UCHIYAMA, Nami OTAKE (46' Kaori NAGAMINE), Akemi NODA. (Coach:
Tamotsu SUZUKI).
Goals: 66' Lena VIDEKULL 1-0, 88' Anneli ANDELÉN 2-0.
Referee: Petros MATHABELA (South Africa) Attendance: 7.811

09.06.1995 Tingvalla IP, Karlstad: Brazil – Germany 1-6 (1-3)
Brazil: Margarete Maria Pioresan "MEG", ELANE dos Santos Rêgo, Rosilane Camargo Mota
"FANTA", SOLANGE Santos Bastos *(YC30)*, SUZY Bitencourt de Oliveira, Sisleide do Amor
Lima "SISSI", VALERIA Aparecida Bonifacio (80' Miraildes Maciel Mota "FORMIGA"),
LEDA MARIA Cozer Abreu *(YC62)* (90' MARCIA TAFFAREL), CENIRA Sampaio do
Prado *(YC25)*, Delma Gonçalves "PRETINHA" (66' TÂNIA Maria Pereira Ribeiro), ROSELI
de Belo. (Coach: ADEMAR FONSECA Júnior).
Germany: Manuela GOLLER, Anouschka BERNHARD, Birgitt AUSTERMÜHL *(YC35)* (46'
Tina WUNDERLICH *(YC65)*), Ursula LOHN, Silva NEID, Maren MEINERT (74' Patricia
BROCKER Grigoli), Martina VOSS-TECKLENBURG, Bettina WIEGMANN (83' Pia
WUNDERLICH), Dagmar POHLMANN, Birgit PRINZ *(YC59)*, Heidi MOHR. (Coach: Gero
BISANZ).
Goals: 5' Birgit PRINZ 0-1, 19' ROSELI de Belo 1-1, 22' Maren MEINERT 1-2, 42' Bettina
WIEGMANN 1-3 (p), 78', 89' Heidi MOHR 1-4, 1-5, 90' Anouschka BERNHARD 1-6.
Referee: Alain HAMER (Luxembourg) Attendance: 3.203

Sent-off: 63' SUZY Bitencourt de Oliveira.

16

Team	Pld	W	D	L	GF	GA	GD	Pts
Germany	*3*	*2*	*0*	*1*	*9*	*4*	*5*	*6*
Sweden	*3*	*2*	*0*	*1*	*5*	*3*	*2*	*6*
Japan	*3*	*1*	*0*	*2*	*2*	*4*	*-2*	*3*
Brazil	*3*	*1*	*0*	*2*	*3*	*8*	*-5*	*3*

GROUP B

06.06.1995   Tingvalla IP, Karlstad: Norway – Nigeria 8-0 (2-0)
Norway: Bente NORDBY, Linda MEDALEN, Anne NYMARK ANDERSEN (77' Nina NYMARK ANDERSEN Jakobsen), Tina SVENSSON, Gro ESPESETH, Merete MYKLEBUST, Hege RIISE (69' Tone Gunn FRUSTØL), Ann Kristin AARØNES, Tone HAUGEN, Heidi STØRE (55' Marianne PETTERSEN), Kristin SANDBERG. (Coach: Even Jostein PELLERUD).
Nigeria: Ann CHIEJINE, Florence OMAGBEMI, Mavis OGUN, Ngozi EZEOCHA *(YC69)* (71' Prisca EMEAFU), Omo-Love BRANCH (73' Nkechi MBILITAM *(YC86)*), Phoebe EBIMIEKUMO, Nkiru OKOSIEME, Ann MUKORO, Mercy AKIDE (46' Patience AVRE), Rita NWADIKE, Adaku OKOROAFOR. (Coach: Paul Ebiye HAMILTON).
Goals: 30', 44' Kristin SANDBERG 1-0, 2-0, 49' Hege RIISE 3-0, 60' Ann Kristin AARØNES 4-0, 67' Linda MEDALEN 5-0, 76' Tina SVENSSON 6-0 (p), 82' Kristin SANDBERG 7-0, 90' Ann Kristin AARØNES 8-0.
Referee: Alain HAMER (Luxembourg)   Attendance: 4.344

06.06.1995   Olympia, Helsingborg: England – Canada 3-2 (0-0)
England: Pauline COPE Boanas, Tina Ann MAPES (70' Hope Patricia POWELL), Samantha BRITTON, Clare Elizabeth TAYLOR, Brenda SEMPARE, Karen BURKE, Gillian COULTARD, Marieanne SPACEY, Deborah (Debbie) BAMPTON, Karen FARLEY *(YC77)*, Karen WALKER (75' Kerry DAVIS). (Coach: Ted COPELAND).
Canada: Carla CHIN, Charmaine HOOPER, Janine HELLAND Wood, Michelle RING, Cathy ROSS (78' Suzanne MUIR), Andrea NEIL, Geraldine DONNELLY *(YC44)*, Veronica O'BRIEN, Angela KELLY, Silvana BURTINI, Helen STOUMBOS *(YC17)*. (Coach: Sylvie BÉLIVEAU).
Goals: 51' Gillian COULTARD 1-0 (p), 76' Marieanne SPACEY 2-0 (p), 85' Gillian COULTARD 3-0, 87' Helen STOUMBOS 3-1, 90+1' Geraldine DONNELLY 3-2.
Referee: Eva ÖDLUND (Sweden)   Attendance: 655

17

08.06.1995 Olympia, Helsingborg: Nigeria – Canada 3-3 (1-2)
Nigeria: Ann CHIEJINE, Yinka KUDAISI, Florence OMAGBEMI, Mavis OGUN, Prisca
EMEAFU, Omo-Love BRANCH (41' Nkechi MBILITAM *(YC83)*), Phoebe EBIMIEKUMO,
Maureen MMADU (60' Ann MUKORO), Patience AVRE *(YC14)*, Rita NWADIKE, Adaku
OKOROAFOR. (Coach: Paul Ebiye HAMILTON).
Canada: Carla CHIN, Charmaine HOOPER, Janine HELLAND Wood, Michelle RING, Luce
MONGRAIN *(YC44)*, Andrea NEIL, Geraldine DONNELLY, Veronica O'BRIEN (61'
Suzanne GERRIOR), Annie CARON (77' Helen STOUMBOS), Angela KELLY, Silvana
BURTINI. (Coach: Sylvie BÉLIVEAU).
Goals: 12' Silvana BURTINI 0-1, 20' Geraldine DONNELLY 0-2, 26' Rita NWADIKE 1-2,
55' Silvana BURTINI 1-3, 60' Patience AVRE 2-3, 77' Adaku OKOROAFOR 3-3.
Referee: Pirom UN PRASERT (Thailand) Attendance: 250

08.06.1995 Tingvalla IP, Karlstad: Norway – England 2-0 (2-0)
Norway: Bente NORDBY, Linda MEDALEN (73' Randi LEINAN), Anne NYMARK
ANDERSEN *(YC34)*, Nina NYMARK ANDERSEN Jakobsen, Tina SVENSSON, Gro
ESPESETH, Merete MYKLEBUST, Hege RIISE (85' Hege GUNNERØD), Ann Kristin
AARØNES, Tone HAUGEN, Kristin SANDBERG (66' Marianne PETTERSEN). (Coach:
Even Jostein PELLERUD).
England: Pauline COPE Boanas, Tina Ann MAPES, Samantha BRITTON (65' Kerry DAVIS),
Clare Elizabeth TAYLOR, Brenda SEMPARE *(YC54)*, Karen BURKE, Gillian COULTARD
(82' Rebecca EASTON), Marieanne SPACEY (36' Hope Patricia POWELL), Deborah
(Debbie) BAMPTON, Karen FARLEY, Karen WALKER. (Coach: Ted COPELAND).
Goals: 7' Tone HAUGEN 1-0, 37' Hege RIISE 2-0.
Referee: Eduardo GAMBOA Martinez (Chile) Attendance: 5.520

10.06.1995 Tingvalla IP, Karlstad: Nigeria – England 2-3 (1-3)
Nigeria: Ann CHIEJINE, Yinka KUDAISI *(YC68)*, Florence OMAGBEMI, Mavis OGUN,
Prisca EMEAFU, Ngozi EZEOCHA (44' Maureen MMADU *(YC90)*), Phoebe EBIMIEKUMO
(YC5), Patience AVRE (47' Nkiru OKOSIEME), Ann MUKORO, Rita NWADIKE, Adaku
OKOROAFOR. (Coach: Paul Ebiye HAMILTON).
England: Lesley HIGGS Shipp, Tina Ann MAPES, Clare Elizabeth TAYLOR (81' Samantha
BRITTON), Brenda SEMPARE (58' Rebecca EASTON), Karen BURKE, Gillian
COULTARD, Marieanne SPACEY (70' Hope Patricia POWELL), Deborah (Debbie)
BAMPTON, Kerry DAVIS, Karen FARLEY, Karen WALKER. (Coach: Ted COPELAND).
Goals: 10' Karen FARLEY 0-1, 13' Adaku OKOROAFOR 1-1, 27' Karen WALKER 1-2,
38' Karen FARLEY 1-3, 74' Rita NWADIKE 2-3.
Referee: Ingrid Jonsson (Sweden) Attendance: 1.843

18

10.06.1995 Strömvallen, Gävle: Norway – Canada 7-0 (3-0)
Norway: Bente NORDBY, Linda MEDALEN (46' Randi LEINAN), Anne NYMARK
ANDERSEN, Tina SVENSSON, Gro ESPESETH, Merete MYKLEBUST, Hege RIISE (46'
Kristin SANDBERG), Ann Kristin AARØNES, Tone HAUGEN (69' Agnete CARLSEN),
Heidi STØRE, Marianne PETTERSEN. (Coach: Even Jostein PELLERUD).
Canada: Carla CHIN, Charmaine HOOPER (YC36), Janine HELLAND Wood, Suzanne MUIR
(85' Andrea NEIL), Michelle RING (YC88), Cathy ROSS, Geraldine DONNELLY (YC80),
Annie CARON (YC26), Angela KELLY, Silvana BURTINI, Helen STOUMBOS. (Coach:
Sylvie BÉLIVEAU).
Goals: 4' Ann Kristin AARØNES 1-0, 12' Hege RIISE 2-0, 21' Ann Kristin AARØNES 3-0,
71' Marianne PETTERSEN 4-0, 84' Randi NEINAN 5-0, 89' Marianne PETTERSEN 6-0,
90+3' Ann Kristin AARØNES 7-0.
Referee: MARIA Edilene SIQUEIRA (Brazil)   Attendance: 2.715

Team	Pld	W	D	L	GF	GA	GD	Pts
Norway	*3*	*3*	*0*	*0*	*17*	*0*	*17*	*9*
England	*3*	*2*	*0*	*1*	*6*	*6*	*0*	*6*
Canada	3	0	1	2	5	13	-8	1
Nigeria	3	0	1	2	5	14	-9	1

GROUP C

06.06.1995 Strömvallen, Gävle: United States – China PR 3-3 (2-1)
United States: Briana Collette SCURRY, Joy Lynn FAWCETT Biefeld, Carla Werden
OVERBECK, Linda HAMILTON, Kristine Marie LILLY Heavey, Tiffany Marie ROBERTS
Sahaydak, Julie Maurine FOUDY, Michelle Anne AKERS (18' Tiffeny Carleen MILBRETT,
76' Holly Jean MANTHEI), Tisha Lea VENTURINI Hoch, Mariel Margaret (Mia) HAMM,
Carin Jennings GABARRA. (Coach: Tony DiCICCO).
China PR: ZHONG Honglian, FAN Yunjie, WANG Liping (YC3), WEN Lirong, NIU Lijie,
ZHAO Lihong, ZHOU Yang, SUN Qingmei (84' SHUI Qingxia), CHEN Yufeng (47' LIU
Ailing), SUN Wen, SHI Guihong (35' WEI Haiying). (Coach: YUANAN Ma).
Goals: 22' Tisha Lea VENTURINI Hoch 1-0, 34' Tiffeny Carleen MILBRETT 2-0,
38' WANG Liping 2-1, 51' Mariel Margaret (Mia) HAMM 3-1, 74' WEI Haiying 3-2,
79' SUN Wen 3-3.
Referee: Ingrid JONSSON (Sweden)   Attendance: 4.635

19

06.06.1995 Arosvallen, Västerås: Denmark – Australia 5-0 (3-0)
Denmark: Dorthe LARSEN Nielsen, Lene TERP, Rikke BRINK Holm, Kamma FLÆNG,
Anne DOT EGGERS NIELSEN, Katrine Søndergaard PEDERSEN (78' Jeanne AXELSEN),
Birgit CHRISTENSEN, Anette LAURSEN *(YC28)* (65' Christina BONDE), Gitte KROGH,
Lene MADSEN (63' Christina HANSEN), Helle JENSEN. (Coach: Keld GANTZHORN).
Australia: Tracey WHEELER, Cheryl SALISBURY *(YC37)* (57' Angela IANNOTTA), Sarah
COOPER, Anissa TANN DARBY, Jane OAKLEY, Sonia GEGENHUBER, Lisa
CASAGRANDE (79' Lizzy CLAYDON), Alison FORMAN *(YC25)*, Julie MURRAY, Sunni
HUGHES (57' Kim LEMBRYK), Michelle WATSON *(YC45)*. (Coach: Tom SERMANNI).
Goals: 12' Gitte KROGH 1-0, 25' Anne DOT EGGERS NIELSEN 2-0,
37' Helle JENSEN 3-0, 48' Gitte KROGH 4-0, 86' Christina HANSEN 5-0.
Referee: Bente Ovedie SKOGVANG (Norway)   Attendance: 1.500

Sent-off: 30' Sonia GEGENHUBER.

08.06.1995 Arosvallen, Västerås: China PR – Australia 4-2 (1-1)
China PR: ZHONG Honglian, FAN Yunjie, WANG Liping, XIE Huilin, ZHAO Lihong, LIU
Ailing, ZHOU Yang *(YC79)*, SHUI Qingxia (27' WEI Haiying), CHEN Yufeng (69' WEN
Lirong), SUN Wen, SHI Guihong. (Coach: YUANAN Ma).
Australia: Tracey WHEELER, Cheryl SALISBURY *(YC73)* (77' Lizzy CLAYDON), Sarah
COOPER, Anissa TANN DARBY, Jane OAKLEY, Angela IANNOTTA, Alison FORMAN,
Kim LEMBRYK *(YC62)* (62' Lisa CASAGRANDE), Julie MURRAY (81' Denie
PENTECOST), Sunni HUGHES, Michelle WATSON *(YC45)*. (Coach: Tom SERMANNI).
Goals: 23' ZHOU Yang 1-0, 25' Angela IANNOTTA 1-1, 54', 78' SHI Guihong 2-1, 3-1,
89' Sunni HUGHES 3-2, 90+3' LIU Ailing 4-2.
Referee: MARIA Edilene SIQUEIRA (Brazil)   Attendance: 1.500

08.06.1995 Strömvallen, Gävle: United States – Denmark 2-0 (1-0)
United States: Briana Collette SCURRY, Joy Lynn FAWCETT Biefeld, Carla Werden
OVERBECK, Linda HAMILTON (53' Thori Yvette STAPLES BRYAN), Kristine Marie
LILLY Heavey, Tiffany Marie ROBERTS Sahaydak, Julie Maurine FOUDY *(YC38)*, Tisha
Lea VENTURINI Hoch, Tiffeny Carleen MILBRETT (61' Debbie KELLER), Mariel
Margaret (Mia) HAMM, Carin Jennings GABARRA (85' Sarah RAFANELLI). (Coach: Tony
DiCICCO).
Denmark: Dorthe LARSEN Nielsen *(YC55)*, Lene TERP, Rikke BRINK Holm, Kamma
FLÆNG, Anne DOT EGGERS NIELSEN, Katrine Søndergaard PEDERSEN, Birgit
CHRISTENSEN, Anette LAURSEN (46' Jeanne AXELSEN), Gitte KROGH (53' Christina
HANSEN), Lene MADSEN (61' Christina PETERSEN *(YC89)*), Helle JENSEN. (Coach: Keld
GANTZHORN).
Goals: 9' Kristine Marie LILLY Heavey 1-0, 49' Tiffeny Carleen MILBRETT 2-0.
Referee: Mamadou Engage CAMARA (Guinea)   Attendance: 2.704

Sent-off: 88' Briana Collette SCURRY.

20

10.06.1995 Arosvallen, Västerås: China PR – Denmark 3-1 (1-1)
China PR: GAO Hong, FAN Yunjie, WANG Liping, XIE Huilin, WEN Lirong, ZHAO
Lihong, LIU Ailing, ZHOU Yang, SUN Wen, WEI Haiying, SHI Guihong (73' SHUI
Qingxia). (Coach: YUANAN Ma).
Denmark: Dorthe LARSEN Nielsen, Lene TERP, Rikke BRINK Holm, Louise HANSEN,
Anne DOT EGGERS NIELSEN *(YC56)*, Katrine Søndergaard PEDERSEN (43' Bettina
ALLENTOFT), Birgit CHRISTENSEN, Gitte KROGH, Lene MADSEN (79' Christina
PETERSEN), Christina HANSEN, Helle JENSEN (26' Christina BONDE). (Coach: Keld
GANTZHORN).
Goals: 21' SHI Guihong 1-0, 44' Christina BONDE 1-1, 76' SUN Wen 2-1,
90' WEI Haiying 3-1.
Referee: Eduardo GAMBOA Martinez (Chile) Attendance: 1.619

10.06.1995 Olympia, Helsingborg: United States – Australia 4-1 (0-0)
United States: Saskia Johanna WEBBER, Joy Lynn FAWCETT Biefeld, Carla Werden
OVERBECK, Thori Yvette STAPLES BRYAN, Linda HAMILTON, Kristine Marie LILLY
Heavey, Tisha Lea VENTURINI Hoch *(YC55)*, Holly Jean MANTHEI (46' Carin Jennings
GABARRA), Amanda Caryl CROMWELL (61' Julie Maurine FOUDY), Tiffeny Carleen
MILBRETT (78' Debbie KELLER), Mariel Margaret (Mia) HAMM. (Coach: Tony
DiCICCO).
Australia: Tracey WHEELER, Sarah COOPER, Anissa TANN DARBY, Jane OAKLEY (75'
Sacha WAINWRIGHT), Sonia GEGENHUBER, Lisa CASAGRANDE (67' Lizzy
CLAYDON), Angela IANNOTTA *(YC82)*, Alison FORMAN *(YC42)*, Kim LEMBRYK (82'
Kaylene JANSSEN), Julie MURRAY *(YC88)*, Sunni HUGHES. (Coach: Tom SERMANNI).
Goals: 54' Lisa CASAGRANDE 0-1, 69' Julie Maurine FOUDY 1-1,
72' Joy Lynn FAWCETT Biefeld 2-1, 90+2' Carla Werden OVERBECK 3-1 (p),
90+4' Debbie KELLER 4-1.
Referee: Pirom UN PRASERT (Thailand) Attendance: 1.105

Team	Pld	W	D	L	GF	GA	GD	Pts
United States	*3*	*2*	*1*	*0*	*9*	*4*	*5*	*7*
China PR	*3*	*2*	*1*	*0*	*10*	*6*	*4*	*7*
Denmark	*3*	*1*	*0*	*2*	*6*	*5*	*1*	*3*
Australia	3	0	0	3	3	13	-10	0

21

QUARTER-FINALS

13.06.1995 Strömvallen, Gävle: Japan – United States 0-4 (0-3)
Japan: Junko OZAWA, Yumi OBE, Rie YAMAKI *(YC72)*, Kae NISHINA, Yumi TOMEI, Maki HANETA, Asako Takemoto TAKAKURA, Futaba KIOKA, Etsuko HANDA (46' Nami OTAKE), Tamaki UCHIYAMA, Akemi NODA. (Coach: Tamotsu SUZUKI).
United States: Briana Collette SCURRY, Joy Lynn FAWCETT Biefeld, Carla Werden OVERBECK, Linda HAMILTON, Kristine Marie LILLY Heavey (68' Thori Yvette STAPLES BRYAN), Tiffany Marie ROBERTS Sahaydak *(YC47)*, Julie Maurine FOUDY, Tisha Lea VENTURINI Hoch (80' Amanda Caryl CROMWELL), Tiffeny Carleen MILBRETT, Mariel Margaret (Mia) HAMM (61' Debbie KELLER), Carin Jennings GABARRA. (Coach: Tony DiCICCO).
Goals: 8', 42' Kristine Marie LILLY Heavey 0-1, 0-2, 45' Tiffeny Carleen MILBRETT 0-3, 80' Tisha Lea VENTURINI Hoch 0-4.
Referee: Eduardo GAMBOA Martinez (Chile) Attendance: 3.756

13.06.1995 Tingvalla IP, Karlstad: Norway – Denmark 3-1 (1-0)
Norway: Bente NORDBY, Linda MEDALEN *(YC23)*, Anne NYMARK ANDERSEN, Tina SVENSSON, Gro ESPESETH, Merete MYKLEBUST, Hege RIISE, Ann Kristin AARØNES (76' Agnete CARLSEN), Tone HAUGEN, Heidi STØRE, Marianne PETTERSEN (84' Randi LEINAN). (Coach: Even Jostein PELLERUD).
Denmark: Dorthe LARSEN Nielsen, Lene TERP, Rikke BRINK Holm *(YC90)*, Kamma FLÆNG, Louise HANSEN (63' Anette LAURSEN), Anne DOT EGGERS NIELSEN, Katrine Søndergaard PEDERSEN, Jeanne AXELSEN (46' Gitte KROGH), Birgit CHRISTENSEN, Lene MADSEN (86' Christina BONDE), Helle JENSEN. (Coach: Keld GANTZHORN).
Goals: 21' Gro ESPESETH 1-0, 64' Linda MEDALEN 2-0, 85' Hege RIISE 3-0, 86' Gitte KROGH 3-1.
Referee: Pirom UN PRASERT (Thailand) Attendance: 4.655

13.06.1995 Arosvallen, Västerås: Germany – England 3-0 (1-0)
Germany: Manuela GOLLER, Sandra MINNERT, Anouschka BERNHARD, Ursula LOHN, Silva NEID, Maren MEINERT (85' Pia WUNDERLICH), Martina VOSS-TECKLENBURG, Bettina WIEGMANN, Dagmar POHLMANN, Birgit PRINZ (67' Patricia BROCKER Grigoli), Heidi MOHR. (Coach: Gero BISANZ).
England: Pauline COPE Boanas, Tina Ann MAPES (79' Louise WALLER), Clare Elizabeth TAYLOR (87' Samantha BRITTON), Brenda SEMPARE *(YC70)*, Karen BURKE, Gillian COULTARD (46' Rebecca EASTON *(YC57)*), Marieanne SPACEY, Deborah (Debbie) BAMPTON, Kerry DAVIS, Karen FARLEY, Karen WALKER. (Coach: Ted COPELAND).
Goals: 41' Martina VOSS-TECKLENBURG 1-0, 55' Maren MEINERT 2-0, 82' Heidi MOHR 3-0.
Referee: Bente Ovedie SKOGVANG (Norway) Attendance: 2.317

13.06.1995 Olympia, Helsingborg: Sweden – China PR 1-1 (0-1, 1-1)
Sweden: Elisabeth LEIDINGE, Gärd Kristin BENGTSSON (65' Annika NESSVOLD), Malin
Elisabeth ANDERSSON, Anna POHJANEN, Lena VIDEKULL, Susanne HEDBERG, Eva
ZEIKFALVY (46' Åsa LÖNNQVIST), Pia Mariane SUNDHAGE, Anneli ANDELÉN (71'
Malin FLINK), Ulrika KALTE, Helen NILSSON. (Coach: Bengt SIMONSSON).
China PR: GAO Hong, FAN Yunjie, WANG Liping (103' SHUI Qingxia), XIE Huilin *(YC22)*,
WEN Lirong, ZHAO Lihong (119' CHEN Yufeng), LIU Ailing *(YC77)*, ZHOU Yang, SUN
Qingmei, SUN Wen, SHI Guihong (51' WEI Haiying). (Coach: YUANAN Ma).
Goals: 29' SUN Qingmei 0-1, 90+3' Ulrika KALTE 1-1.
Referee: Sonia DENONCOURT (Canada) Attendance: 7.537

Penalties: SUN Wen 0-1, Malin Elisabeth ANDERSSON missed, XIE Huilin 0-2,
Lena VIDEKULL 1-2, CHEN Yufeng 1-3, Anna POHJANEN 2-3, SHUI
Qingxia 2-4, Pia Mariane SUNDHAGE 3-4, LIU Ailing missed, Annika
NESSVOLD missed.

China PR qualified after winning 4-3 on penalties.

SEMI-FINALS

15.06.1995 Arosvallen, Västerås: United States – Norway 0-1 (0-1)
United States: Briana Collette SCURRY, Joy Lynn FAWCETT Biefeld, Carla Werden
OVERBECK, Linda HAMILTON, Kristine Marie LILLY Heavey, Tiffany Marie ROBERTS
Sahaydak (53' Tiffeny Carleen MILBRETT), Julie Maurine FOUDY, Michelle Anne AKERS,
Tisha Lea VENTURINI Hoch, Mariel Margaret (Mia) HAMM, Carin Jennings GABARRA.
(Coach: Tony DiCICCO).
Norway: Bente NORDBY, Linda MEDALEN, Anne NYMARK ANDERSEN, Nina
NYMARK ANDERSEN Jakobsen, Tina SVENSSON *(YC6)*, Gro ESPESETH, Merete
MYKLEBUST, Hege RIISE, Ann Kristin AARØNES, Tone HAUGEN (69' Marianne
PETTERSEN), Heidi STØRE. (Coach: Even Jostein PELLERUD).
Goal: 10' Ann Kristin AARØNES 0-1.
Referee: Alain HAMER (Luxembourg) Attendance: 2.893

Sent-off: 76' Heidi STØRE.

15.06.1995 Olympia, Helsingborg: Germany – China PR 1-0 (0-0)
Germany: Manuela GOLLER, Anouschka BERNHARD, Birgitt AUSTERMÜHL, Ursula
LOHN, Silva NEID, Maren MEINERT, Martina VOSS-TECKLENBURG, Bettina
WIEGMANN, Dagmar POHLMANN, Birgit PRINZ (83' Pia WUNDERLICH), Heidi MOHR.
(Coach: Gero BISANZ).
China PR: GAO Hong, FAN Yunjie (86' CHEN Yufeng), WANG Liping, XIE Huilin, WEN
Lirong *(YC52)*, ZHAO Lihong, LIU Ailing, ZHOU Yang, SUN Qingmei, SUN Wen, SHI
Guihong *(YC65)*. (Coach: YUANAN Ma).
Goal: 88' Bettina WIEGMANN 1-0.
Referee: Petros MATHABELA (South Africa) Attendance: 3.693

23

THIRD PLACE MATCH

17.06.1995 Strömvallen, Gävle: China PR – United States 0-2 (0-1)
China PR: GAO Hong, FAN Yunjie (72' CHEN Yufeng), WANG Liping, XIE Huilin *(YC45)*,
WEN Lirong, NIU Lijie, ZHAO Lihong, LIU Ailing, SUN Qingmei, SUN Wen (59' WEI
Haiying), SHI Guihong. (Coach: YUANAN Ma).
United States: Briana Collette SCURRY, Joy Lynn FAWCETT Biefeld, Carla Werden
OVERBECK, Thori Yvette STAPLES BRYAN, Linda HAMILTON (54' Tiffany Marie
ROBERTS Sahaydak), Kristine Marie LILLY Heavey, Julie Maurine FOUDY, Tisha Lea
VENTURINI Hoch, Tiffeny Carleen MILBRETT (68' Debbie KELLER), Mariel Margaret
(Mia) HAMM, Carin Jennings GABARRA (80 Sarah RAFANELLI). (Coach: Tony
DiCICCO).
Goals: 24' Tisha Lea VENTURINI Hoch 0-1, 55' Mariel Margaret (Mia) HAMM 0-2.
Referee: Sonia DENONCOURT (Canada) Attendance: 4.335

FINAL

18.06.1995 Råsundastadion, Solna: Germany –Norway 0-2 (0-2)
Germany: Manuela GOLLER, Anouschka BERNHARD *(YC2)*, Birgitt AUSTERMÜHL,
Ursula LOHN, Silva NEID, Maren MEINERT (86' Sandra SMISEK), Martina VOSS-
TECKLENBURG, Bettina WIEGMANN, Dagmar POHLMANN (75' Pia WUNDERLICH),
Birgit PRINZ (83' Patricia BROCKER Grigoli), Heidi MOHR. (Coach: Gero BISANZ).
Norway: Bente NORDBY, Linda MEDALEN *(YC58)*, Anne NYMARK ANDERSEN *(YC22)*,
Nina NYMARK ANDERSEN Jakobsen, Tina SVENSSON, Gro ESPESETH, Merete
MYKLEBUST, Hege RIISE, Ann Kristin AARØNES *(YC70)*, Tone HAUGEN, Marianne
PETTERSEN. (Coach: Even Jostein PELLERUD).
Goals: 37' Hege RIISE 0-1, 40' Marianne PETTERSEN 0-2.
Referee: Ingrid JONSSON (Sweden) Attendance: 17.158

Norway won the World Cup.

24

FIFA WOMEN'S WORLD CUP – USA 1999

GROUP STAGE

GROUP A

19.06.1999 Giants Stadium, East Rutherford: United States – Denmark 3-0 (1-0)
United States: Briana Collette SCURRY, Kathryn Michele MARKGRAF Sobrero, Joy Lynn FAWCETT Biefeld, Carla Werden OVERBECK, Kristine Marie LILLY Heavey, Brandi Denise CHASTAIN, Julie Maurine FOUDY, Michelle Anne AKERS, Tiffeny Carleen MILBRETT (82' Shannon Ann MACMILLAN), Mariel Margaret (Mia) HAMM, Cynthia Marie (Cindy) PARLOW Cone. (Coach: Tony DiCICCO).
Denmark: Dorthe LARSEN Nielsen, Karina CHRISTENSEN, Lene TERP, Katrine Søndergaard PEDERSEN, Jeanne AXELSEN, Janne RASMUSSEN *(YC11)*, Christina PETERSEN (83' Lise SØNDERGAARD), Lene REVSBECK JENSEN (78' Louise HANSEN), Merete PEDERSEN, Gitte KROGH, Mikka HANSEN (63' Janni LUND JOHANSEN). (Coach: Jørgen HVIDEMOSE).
Goals: 17' Mariel Margaret (Mia) HAMM 1-0, 73' Julie Maurine FOUDY 2-0, 89' Kristine Marie LILLY Heavey 3-0
Referee: Sonia DENONCOURT (Canada)   Attendance: 78.972

21.06.1999 Rose Bowl, Pasadena: Korea DPR – Nigeria 1-2 (0-0)
Korea DPR: KYE Yong-Sun, YUN In-Sil, KIM Sun-Hui (61' JO Jong-Ran), KIM Hye-Ran, RI Ae-Gyong, RI Hyang-Ok *(YC1)*, SOL Yong-Suk (55' RI Kyong-Ae), KIM Kum-Sil (29' PAK Jong-Ae), RI Kum-Suk *(YC5)*, JIN Pyol-Hui *(YC88)*, JO Song-Ok. (Coach: TONG Chan).
Nigeria: Ann CHIEJINE, Yinka KUDAISI (86' Adanna NWANERI *(YC88)*), Florence Kikelomo AJAYI, Florence OMAGBEMI, Eberechi OPARA *(YC81)*, Prisca EMEAFU, Nkiru OKOSIEME, Patience AVRE, Ifeanyi CHIEJINE (70' Nkechi EGBE), Mercy AKIDE *(YC90+3)*, Rita NWADIKE. (Coach: Mabo ISMAILA).
Goals: 50' Mercy AKIDE 0-1, 74' JO Song-Ok 1-1, 79' Rita NWADIKE 1-2.
Referee: Katriina ELOVIRTA (Finland)   Attendance: 17.100

25.06.1999 Providence Park, Portland: Korea DPR – Denmark 3-1 (2-0)
Korea DPR: KYE Yong-Sun, YUN In-Sil, KIM Sun-Hui *(YC34)* (46' KIM Hye-Ran), RI Ae-Gyong, RI Hyang-Ok, SOL Yong-Suk, KIM Kum-Sil, PAK Jong-Ae *(YC49,RC86)*, RI Kum-Suk *(YC81)*, JIN Pyol-Hui, JO Song-Ok *(YC83)*. (Coach: TONG Chan).
Denmark: Dorthe LARSEN Nielsen, Marlene KRISTENSEN (9' Hanne SAND CHRISTENSEN), Lene TERP *(YC36)*, Louise HANSEN, Katrine Søndergaard PEDERSEN, Jeanne AXELSEN, Janne RASMUSSEN, Christina PETERSEN, Lene REVSBECK JENSEN (46' Janni LUND JOHANSEN), Merete PEDERSEN (63' Mikka HANSEN), Gitte KROGH. (Coach: Jørgen HVIDEMOSE).
Goals: 15' JIN Pyol-Hui 1-0, 39' JO Song-Ok 2-0, 73' KIM Kum-Sil 3-0, 74' Janni LUND JOHANSEN 3-1.
Referee: Martha TORO (Colombia)   Attendance: 20.129

Sent-off: 86' PAK Jong-Ae.

25.06.1999   Soldier Field, Chicago: United States – Nigeria 7-1 (6-1)
United States: Briana Collette SCURRY, Kathryn Michele MARKGRAF Sobrero (46' Sara
Eve WHALEN Hess), Joy Lynn FAWCETT Biefeld, Carla Werden OVERBECK, Kristine
Marie LILLY Heavey, Brandi Denise CHASTAIN, Julie Maurine FOUDY, Michelle Anne
AKERS (46' Lorraine Ming (Lorrie) FAIR), Tiffeny Carleen MILBRETT, Mariel Margaret
(Mia) HAMM (57' Shannon Ann MACMILLAN), Cynthia Marie (Cindy) PARLOW Cone.
(Coach: Tony DiCICCO).
Nigeria: Ann CHIEJINE, Yinka KUDAISI, Florence Kikelomo AJAYI *(YC45)*, Florence
OMAGBEMI, Eberechi OPARA, Prisca EMEAFU (84' Gloria USIETA), Nkiru OKOSIEME,
Patience AVRE *(YC30)* (53' Stella MBACHU), Ifeanyi CHIEJINE (43' Nkechi EGBE), Mercy
AKIDE, Rita NWADIKE. (Coach: Mabo ISMAILA).
Goals: 2' Ifeanyi CHIEJINE 1-0 (og), 3' Nkiru OKOSIEME 1-1, 20' Mariel Margaret (Mia)
HAMM 2-1, 23' Tiffeny Carleen MILBRETT 3-1, 32' Kristine Marie LILLY Heavey 4-1,
39' Michelle Anne AKERS 5-1, 42' Cynthia Marie (Cindy) PARLOW Cone 6-1,
83' Tiffeny Carleen MILBRETT 7-1.
Referee: Nicole PETIGNAT (Switzerland)   Attendance: 65.080

27.06.1999   FedEx Field, Landover: Nigeria – Denmark 2-0 (1-0)
Nigeria: Ann CHIEJINE, Yinka KUDAISI, Florence OMAGBEMI, Eberechi OPARA, Prisca
EMEAFU *(YC90+1)*, Nkiru OKOSIEME, Patience AVRE, Ifeanyi CHIEJINE (81' Adanna
NWANERI), Mercy AKIDE, Nkechi EGBE (54' Stella MBACHU *(YC88)*), Rita NWADIKE.
(Coach: Mabo ISMAILA).
Denmark: Dorthe LARSEN Nielsen, Lene TERP, Katrine Søndergaard PEDERSEN, Jeanne
AXELSEN, Janne RASMUSSEN, Christina PETERSEN, Janni LUND JOHANSEN, Hanne
SAND CHRISTENSEN, Mikka HANSEN (58' Merete PEDERSEN), Hanne NØRREGAARD
(32' Lene REVSBECK JENSEN), Gitte KROGH *(YC50)* (66' Louise HANSEN). (Coach:
Jørgen HVIDEMOSE).
Goals: 25' Mercy AKIDE 1-0, 81' Nkiru OKOSIEME 2-0.
Referee: MARIA Edilene SIQUEIRA (Brazil)   Attendance: 22.109

28.06.1999   Foxboro Stadium, Fosborough: United States – Korea DPR 3-0 (0-0)
United States: Briana Collette SCURRY, Joy Lynn FAWCETT Biefeld, Carla Werden
OVERBECK, Sara Eve WHALEN Hess, Kristine Marie LILLY Heavey, Brandi Denise
CHASTAIN, Tiffany Marie ROBERTS Sahaydak (73' Christie PEARCE), Tisha Lea
VENTURINI Hoch, Shannon Ann MACMILLAN, Mariel Margaret (Mia) HAMM (46'
Tiffeny Carleen MILBRETT), Cynthia Marie (Cindy) PARLOW Cone (46' Julie Maurine
FOUDY). (Coach: Tony DiCICCO).
Korea DPR: KYE Yong-Sun, YUN In-Sil, KIM Sun-Hui, KIM Sun-Hye *(YC8)*, KIM Hye-
Ran, RI Ae-Gyong (71' YANG Kyong-Hui), RI Hyang-Ok, SOL Yong-Suk, KIM Kum-Sil
(YC74), JIN Pyol-Hui (61' JO Jong-Ran), JO Song-Ok *(YC24)*. (Coach: TONG Chan).
Goals: 56' Shannon Ann MACMILLAN 1-0, 68', 76' Tisha Lea VENTURINI Hoch 2-0, 3-0.
Referee: Katriina ELOVIRTA (Finland)   Attendance: 50.484

Team	Pld	W	D	L	GF	GA	GD	Pts
United States	3	3	0	0	13	1	12	9
Nigeria	3	2	0	1	5	8	-3	6
Korea DPR	3	1	0	2	4	6	-2	3
Denmark	3	0	0	3	1	8	-7	0

GROUP B

19.06.1999   Giants Stadium, East Rutherford: Brazil – Mexico 7-1 (5-1)
Brazil: Marlisa Wahlbrink "MARAVILHA", Alissandra Cavalcante "NENÊ", ELANE dos Santos Rego, SUZANA Ferreira da Silva, Rosilane Camargo Mota "FANTA" (82' JULIANA Ribeiro Cabral), MARISA Pires Nogueira, Sisleide do Amor Lima "SISSI", Maria Dias Aparecida de Souza "CIDINHA" (46' ANDRÉIA dos Santos), RAQUEL de Souza Noronha, Delma Gonçalves "PRETINHA", KÁTIA Cilene Teixeira da Silva (72' Miraildes Maciel Mota "FORMIGA"). (Coach: WILSON DE OLIVEIRA Riça).
Mexico: Linnea Andrea QUIÑONES Sandland, Susana MORA Chávez, Martha Ofelia MOORE Camacho (73' Patricia PÉREZ Peña), Regina Marie OCEGUERA Schmul, Fátima LEYVA Morán (46' Laurie Anne HILL Rozenel), Andrea RODEBAUGH Huitrón, María del Carmen Denise IRETA Gonzalez *(YC4)*, Maribel Guadalupe DOMÍNGUEZ Castelán *(YC74)*, Lisa Anne NÁÑEZ Stromberg *(YC53)*, Mónica Marie GERARDO Moran (78' Iris Adriana MORA Vallejo *(YC81)*), Mónica Christine GONZÁLEZ Canales. (Coach: Leonardo CUÉLLAR Rivera).
Goals: 3' Delma Gonçalves "PRETINHA" 1-0, 10' Maribel Guadalupe DOMÍNGUEZ Castelán 1-1, 12' Delma Gonçalves "PRETINHA" 2-1, 29' Sisleide Amor Lima "SISSI" 3-1, 35' KÁTIA Cilene Teixeira da Silva 4-1 (p), 42', 50' Sisleide do Amor Lima "SISSI" 5-1, 6-1, 90+1' Delma Gonçalves "PRETINHA" 7-1.
Referee: Nicole PETIGNAT (Switzerland)   Attendance: 78.972

20.06.1999   Rose Bowl, Pasadena: Germany – Italy 1-1 (0-1)
Germany: Silke ROTTENBERG, Kerstin STEGEMANN, Doris FITSCHEN, Ariane HINGST, Stephanie JONES, Pia WUNDERLICH, Maren MEINERT (82' Monika MEYER), Bettina WIEGMANN, Birgit PRINZ, Inka GRINGS, Sandra SMISEK (86' Renate LINGOR). (Coach: Tina THEUNE).
Italy: Giorgia BRENZAN, Roberta STEFANELLI, Daniela TAVALAZZI, Luisa MARCHIO, Anna DUO, Adele FROLLANI (71' Paola ZANNI), Manuela TESSE (68' Damiana DE IANA), Federica D'ASTOLFO *(YC32)*, Antonella CARTA, Patrizia PANICO, Rita GUARINO (89' Silvia FIORINI). (Coach: Carlo FACCHIN).
Goals: 36' Patrizia PANICO 0-1, 61' Bettina WIEGMANN 1-1 (p).
Referee: Bola ABIDOYE (Nigeria)   Attendance: 17.100

27

24.06.1999   Soldier Field, Chicago: Brazil – Italy 2-0 (1-0)
Brazil: Marlisa Wahlbrink "MARAVILHA", TÂNIA Maria Pereira Ribeiro *(YC74)*, Alissandra
Cavalcante "NENÊ" *(YC84)* (89' JULIANA Ribeiro Cabral), ELANE dos Santos Rego,
SUZANA Ferreira da Silva *(YC35)*, MARISA Pires Nogueira, Sisleide do Amor Lima "SISSI",
Maria Dias Aparecida de Souza "CIDINHA", RAQUEL de Souza Noronha (46' Miraildes
Maciel Mota "FORMIGA"), Delma Gonçalves "PRETINHA", KÁTIA Cilene Teixeira da
Silva (75' ANDRÉIA dos Santos). (Coach: WILSON DE OLIVEIRA Riça).
Italy: Giorgia BRENZAN, Roberta STEFANELLI, Daniela TAVALAZZI, Luisa MARCHIO,
Anna DUO *(YC13)*, Adele FROLLANI (55' Damiana DE IANA), Manuela TESSE, Federica
D'ASTOLFO *(YC21)*, Antonella CARTA (58' Silvia FIORINI), Patrizia PANICO, Rita
GUARINO *(YC71)* (74' Silvia TAGLIACARNE). (Coach: Carlo FACCHIN).
Goals: 3', 63' Sisleide do Amor Lima "SISSI" 1-0, 2-0.
Referee: Gitte NIELSEN (Denmark)   Attendance: 65.080

25.06.1999   Providence Park, Portland: Germany – Mexico 6-0 2-0)
Germany: Silke ROTTENBERG, Sandra MINNERT, Doris FITSCHEN, Ariane HINGST,
Stephanie JONES, Pia WUNDERLICH, Maren MEINERT *(YC21)* (64' Renate LINGOR),
Bettina WIEGMANN (69' Melanie HOFFMANN), Birgit PRINZ (75' Claudia MÜLLER),
Inka GRINGS, Sandra SMISEK. (Coach: Tina THEUNE).
Mexico: Linnea Andrea QUIÑONES Sandland, Susana MORA Chávez, Regina Marie
OCEGUERA Schmul, Fátima LEYVA Morán, Mónica VERGARA Rubio (62' Mónica Marie
GERARDO Moran), Patricia PÉREZ Peña, Andrea RODEBAUGH Huitrón (57' Mónica
Christine GONZÁLEZ Canales), Laurie Anne HILL Rozenel, María del Carmen Denise
IRETA Gonzalez, Maribel Guadalupe DOMÍNGUEZ Castelán, Lisa Anne NÁÑEZ Stromberg.
(Coach: Leonardo CUÉLLAR Rivera).
Goals: 10' Inka GRINGS 1-0, 45+1' Sandra SMISEK 2-0, 49' Ariane HINGST 3-0,
57' Inka GRINGS 4-0, 89' Renate LINGOR 5-0, 90+2' Inka GRINGS 6-0.
Referee: IM Eun-Ju (Korea Republic)   Attendance: 20.129

27.06.1999   FedEx Field, Landover: Germany – Brazil 3-3 (1-2)
Germany: Silke ROTTENBERG, Sandra MINNERT *(YC68)*, Doris FITSCHEN, Ariane
HINGST, Stephanie JONES, Pia WUNDERLICH (46' Tina WUNDERLICH *(YC85)*), Maren
MEINERT, Martina VOSS-TECKLENBURG (29' Sandra SMISEK), Bettina WIEGMANN,
Birgit PRINZ, Inka GRINGS (89' Monika MEYER). (Coach: Tina THEUNE).
Brazil: Marlisa Wahlbrink "MARAVILHA", TÂNIA Maria Pereira Ribeiro, Alissandra
Cavalcante "NENÊ", ELANE dos Santos Rego, SUZANA Ferreira da Silva (65' ANDRÉIA
dos Santos), MARISA Pires Nogueira (33' Rosilane Camargo Mota "FANTA"), Sisleide do
Amor Lima "SISSI", Maria Dias Aparecida de Souza "CIDINHA", RAQUEL de Souza
Noronha (60' Miraildes Maciel Mota "FORMIGA" *(YC79)*), Delma Gonçalves "PRETINHA",
KÁTIA Cilene Teixeira da Silva. (Coach: WILSON DE OLIVEIRA Riça).
Goals: 8' Birgit PRINZ 1-0, 15' KÁTIA Cilene Teixeira da Silva 1-1, 20' Sisleide do Amor
Lima "SISSI" 1-2, 46' Bettina WIEGMANN 2-2 (p), 58' Stephanie JONES 3-2,
90+4' ANDRÉIA dos Santos 3-3.
Referee: IM Eun-Ju (Korea Republic)   Attendance: 22.109

28

27.06.1999   Foxboro Stadium, Foxborough: Mexico – Italy 0-2 (0-1)
Mexico: Linnea Andrea QUIÑONES Sandland, Susana MORA Chávez, Martha Ofelia
MOORE Camacho (42' Mónica Christine GONZÁLEZ Canales), Regina Marie OCEGUERA
Schmul, Fátima LEYVA Morán (66' María del Carmen Denise IRETA Gonzalez), Mónica
VERGARA Rubio (55' Laurie Anne HILL Rozenel), Patricia PÉREZ Peña, Andrea
RODEBAUGH Huitrón *(YC74)*, Maribel Guadalupe DOMÍNGUEZ Castelán, Lisa Anne
NÁÑEZ Stromberg, Mónica Marie GERARDO Moran. (Coach: Leonardo CUÉLLAR Rivera).
Italy: Giorgia BRENZAN, Daniela TAVALAZZI, Paola ZANNI, Luisa MARCHIO, Anna
DUO (46' Roberta STEFANELLI), Adele FROLLANI, Alessandra PALLOTTI, Tatiana
ZORRI, Damiana DE IANA, Patrizia PANICO, Rita GUARINO (46' Silvia
TAGLIACARNE). (Coach: Carlo FACCHIN).
Goals: 37' Patrizia PANICO 0-1, 51' Paola ZANNI 0-2.
Referee: Bola ABIDOYE (Nigeria)   Attendance: 50.484

Team	Pld	W	D	L	GF	GA	GD	Pts
Brazil	*3*	*2*	*1*	*0*	*12*	*4*	*8*	*7*
Germany	*3*	*1*	*2*	*1*	*10*	*4*	*6*	*5*
Italy	3	1	1	1	3	3	0	4
Mexico	3	0	0	3	1	15	-14	0

GROUP C

20.06.1999   Spartan Stadium, San Jose: Japan – Canada 1-1 (0-1)
Japan: Nozomi YAMAGO, Hiromi ISOZAKI, Kae NISHINA, Yumi TOMEI, Ayumi HARA,
Tomomi MIYAMOTO, Tomoe KATO, Homare SAWA, Tamaki UCHIYAMA, Nami
OTAKE, Mito ISAKA (52' Yayoi KOBAYASHI). (Coach: Satoshi MIYAUCHI).
Canada: Nicole (Nicci) WRIGHT, Sharolta Louisa NONEN, Isabelle MORNEAU, Charmaine
HOOPER *(YC5)*, Janine HELLAND Wood, Amy Heather WALSH, Tanya FRANCK,
Geraldine DONNELLY, Silvana BURTINI (55' Andrea NEIL), Shannon ROSENOW, Isabelle
HARVEY. (Coach: Neil TURNBULL).
Goals: 32' Silvana BURTINI 0-1, 64' Nami OTAKE 1-1.
Referee: MARIA Edilene SIQUEIRA (Brazil)   Attendance: 23.298

20.06.1999   Foxboro Stadium, Foxborough: Norway – Russia 2-1 (1-0)
Norway: Bente NORDBY, Brit SANDAUNE, Gøril KRINGEN, Linda MEDALEN, Anne
NYMARK ANDERSEN, Unni LEHN (61' Tone Gunn FRUSTØL), Hege RIISE, Monica
KNUDSEN (86' Anita RAPP), Silje JØRGENSEN, Ragnhild Øren GULBRANDSEN (74'
Dagny MELLGREN), Marianne PETTERSEN. (Coach: Per-Mathias HØGMO).
Russia: Svetlana PETKO, Marina BURAKOVA, Natalia FILIPPOVA, Tatiana CHEVERDA,
Natalia BARBASHINA, Natalia KARASEVA, Tatiana EGOROVA, Alexandra
SVETLITSKAYA (84' Elena FOMINA), Olga KARASSEVA (46' Galina KOMAROVA),
Irina GRIGORIEVA, Olga LETYUSHOVA (73' Larissa SAVINA). (Coach: Yuri
BYSTRITSKIY).
Goals: 28' Brit SANDAUNE 1-0, 68' Marianne PETTERSEN 2-0,
78' Galina KOMAROVA 2-1.
Referee: ZUO Xiudi (China PR)   Attendance: 14.873

24.06.1999   FedEx Field, Landover: Norway – Canada 7-1 (2-1)
Norway: Bente NORDBY, Brit SANDAUNE, Gøril KRINGEN (YC45+1), Linda MEDALEN,
Anne NYMARK ANDERSEN (46' Tone Gunn FRUSTØL), Unni LEHN (70' Solveig
GULBRANDSEN), Hege RIISE, Monica KNUDSEN (62'Linda ØRMEN), Silje
JØRGENSEN, Ann Kristin AARØNES, Marianne PETTERSEN. (Coach: Per-Mathias
HØGMO).
Canada: Nicole (Nicci) WRIGHT, Sharolta Louisa NONEN, Isabelle MORNEAU, Charmaine
HOOPER (YC5), Janine HELLAND Wood, Amy Heather WALSH, Tanya FRANCK,
Geraldine DONNELLY, Jeanette HAAS (16' Andrea NEIL), Shannon ROSENOW (70' Mary
Beth BOWIE), Isabelle HARVEY. (Coach: Neil TURNBULL).
Goals: 8' Ann Kristin AARØNES 1-0, 31' Charmaine HOOPER 1-1, 36' Ann Kristin
AARØNES 2-1, 49' Unni LEHN 3-1, 54' Hege RIISE 4-1, 68' Linda MEDALEN
5-1, 76' Marianne PETTERSEN 6-1, 87' Ragnhild Øren GULBRANDSEN 7-1.
Referee: Tammy Nicole OGSTON (Australia)   Attendance: 16.448

24.06.1999   Providence Park, Portland: Japan – Russia 0-5 (0-1)
Japan: Nozomi YAMAGO, Hiromi ISOZAKI, Kae NISHINA, Yumi TOMEI, Ayumi HARA,
Tomomi MIYAMOTO, Tomoe KATO (69' Rie YAMAKI), Homare SAWA (YC72), Tamaki
UCHIYAMA, Nami OTAKE (57' Miyuki YANAGITA), Mito ISAKA (64' Yayoi
KOBAYASHI). (Coach: Satoshi MIYAUCHI).
Russia: Svetlana PETKO, Marina BURAKOVA, Natalia FILIPPOVA, Tatiana CHEVERDA,
Natalia KARASEVA, Galina KOMAROVA, Tatiana EGOROVA (79' Elena FOMINA),
Alexandra SVETLITSKAYA (46' Olga KARASSEVA), Irina GRIGORIEVA, Olga
LETYUSHOVA, Larissa SAVINA (72' Natalia BARBASHINA). (Coach: Yuri
BYSTRITSKIY).
Goals: 29' Larissa SAVINA 0-1, 52' Olga LETYUSHOVA 0-2, 58' Natalia KARASEVA 0-3,
80' Natalia BARBASHINA 0-4, 90' Olga LETYUSHOVA 0-5.
Referee: Sandra HUNT (United States)   Attendance: 17.668

26.06.1999   Giants Stadium, East Rutherford: Canada – Russia 1-4 (0-0)
Canada: Nicole (Nicci) WRIGHT, Sharolta Louisa NONEN, Isabelle MORNEAU, Charmaine
HOOPER, Janine HELLAND Wood, Amy Heather WALSH, Tanya FRANCK *(YC32)*,
Geraldine DONNELLY, Mary Beth BOWIE (55' Silvana BURTINI), Shannon ROSENOW
(80' Sarah MAGLIO), Isabelle HARVEY *(YC49)*. (Coach: Neil TURNBULL).
Russia: Svetlana PETKO, Marina BURAKOVA, Natalia FILIPPOVA, Tatiana CHEVERDA
(72' Yulia YUSHEKIVITCH), Natalia BARBASHINA (56' Larissa SAVINA), Natalia
KARASEVA *(YC77)*, Galina KOMAROVA, Tatiana EGOROVA (61' Elena FOMINA), Olga
KARASSEVA, Irina GRIGORIEVA, Olga LETYUSHOVA. (Coach: Yuri BYSTRITSKIY).
Goals: 54' Irina GRIGORIEVA 0-1, 66' Elena FOMINA 0-2, 76' Charmaine HOOPER 1-2,
86' Elena FOMINA 1-3, 90+1' Olga KARASSEVA1-4.
Referee: ZUO Xiudi (China PR)   Attendance: 29.401

27.06.1999   Soldier Field, Chicago: Norway – Japan 4-0 (3-0)
Norway: Bente NORDBY, Brit SANDAUNE, Anne TØNNESSEN *(YC83)*, Linda MEDALEN
(11' Gøril KRINGEN, 57' Henriette VIKER), Unni LEHN, Hege RIISE, Monica KNUDSEN,
Silje JØRGENSEN *(YC73)*, Tone Gunn FRUSTØL, Ann Kristin AARØNES (38' Solveig
GULBRANDSEN), Dagny MELLGREN. (Coach: Per-Mathias HØGMO).
Japan: Nozomi YAMAGO, Hiromi ISOZAKI, Rie YAMAKI, Kae NISHINA, Yumi TOMEI,
Ayumi HARA (86' Kozue ANDO), Tomomi MIYAMOTO, Homare SAWA *(YC65)*, Tamaki
UCHIYAMA (78' Miyuki YANAGITA), Nami OTAKE, Mito ISAKA (60' Yayoi
KOBAYASHI). (Coach: Satoshi MIYAUCHI).
Goals: 8' Hege RIISE 1-0 (p), 26' Hiromi ISO 2-0 (og), 36' Ann Kristin AARØNES 3-0,
61' Dagny MELLGREN 4-0.
Referee: Marisela CONTRERAS (Venezuela)   Attendance: 34.256

Team	Pld	W	D	L	GF	GA	GD	Pts
Norway	*3*	*3*	*0*	*0*	*13*	*2*	*11*	*9*
Russia	*3*	*2*	*0*	*1*	*10*	*3*	*7*	*6*
Canada	3	0	1	2	3	12	-9	1
Japan	3	0	1	2	1	19	-9	1

31

GROUP D

19.06.1999 Spartan Stadium, San Jose: China PR – Sweden 2-1 (1-1)
China PR: GAO Hong, FAN Yunjie, WANG Liping, XIE Huilin (59' ZHANG Ouying), WEN
Lirong, ZHAO Lihong, LIU Ying, LIU Ailing, BAI Jie, SUN Wen (74' PU Wei), JIN Yan.
(Coach: YUANAN Ma).
Sweden: Ulrika KARLSSON, Karolina WESTBERG, Jane TÖRNQVIST, Gärd Kristin
BENGTSSON (88' Tina NORDLUND), Åsa LÖNNQVIST, Cecilia SANDELL, Malin Sofi
MOSTRÖM (77' Linda FAGERSTRÖM), Malin Elisabeth ANDERSSON, Hanna Carolina
LJUNGBERG, Victoria Margareta Sandell SVENSSON, Therese LUNDIN (46' Malin
GUSTAFSSON). (Coach: Marika Susan DOMANSKI LYFORS).
Goals: 2' Gärd Kristin BENGTSSON 0-1, 17' JIN Yan 1-1, 69' LIU Ailing 2-1.
Referee: Virginia TOVAR Dias (Mexico)   Attendance: 23.298

20.06.1999 Foxboro Stadium, Foxborough: Australia – Ghana 1-1 (0-0)
Australia: Tracey WHEELER, Dianne ALAGICH, Cheryl SALISBURY, Bridgette STARR,
Sarah COOPER, Traci BARTLETT *(YC89)*, Joanne PETERS (89' Kelly GOLEBIOWSKI),
Sharon BLACK, Angela IANNOTTA (59' Lisa CASAGRANDE *(YC65)*), Alison FORMAN,
Julie MURRAY. (Coach: Greg BROWN).
Ghana: Memunatu SULEMANA, Patience SACKEY, Elizabeth BAIDU, Rita YEBOAH
(YC11), Regina ANSAH *(YC4)*, Adjoa BAYOR (79' Lydia ANKRAH), Genevive CLOTTEY
(YC80), Barikisu TETTEY QUAO *(RC26)*, Alberta SACKEY *(YC15)*, Mavis DGAJMAH (32'
Sheila OKAI, 65' Nana GYAMFUAH), Vivian MENSAH. (Coach: Emmanuel AFRANI).
Goals: 74' Julie MURRAY 1-0, 76' Nana GYAMFUAH 1-1.
Referee: Kari SEITZ (United States)   Attendance: 14.873

Sent-off: 26' Barikisu TETTEY QUAO.

24.06.1999 FedEx Field, Landover: Australia – Sweden 1-3 (1-2)
Australia: Bellinda KITCHING, Dianne ALAGICH, Cheryl SALISBURY, Bridgette STARR
(87' Anissa TANN DARBY), Sarah COOPER (76' Angela IANNOTTA), Traci BARTLETT,
Joanne PETERS, Sharon BLACK (58' Kelly GOLEBIOWSKI *(YC79)*), Lisa CASAGRANDE,
Alison FORMAN *(YC85)*, Julie MURRAY. (Coach: Greg BROWN).
Sweden: Ulrika KARLSSON, Karolina WESTBERG, Jane TÖRNQVIST (75' Jessika
SUNDH), Gärd Kristin BENGTSSON *(YC53)* (57' Therese LUNDIN), Åsa LÖNNQVIST,
Cecilia SANDELL, Malin Sofi MOSTRÖM, Malin Elisabeth ANDERSSON, Linda GREN
(46' Malin GUSTAFSSON), Hanna Carolina LJUNGBERG, Victoria Margareta Sandell
SVENSSON. (Coach: Marika Susan DOMANSKI LYFORS).
Goals: 8' Jane TÖRNQVIST 0-1, 21' Hanna Carolina LJUNGBERG 0-2,
32' Julie MURRAY 1-2, 69' Hanna Carolina LJUNGBERG 1-3.
Referee: Fatou GAYE (Senegal)   Attendance: 16.448

24.06.1999   Providence Park, Portland: China PR – Ghana 7-0 (3-0)
China PR: GAO Hong, PU Wei (73' XIE Huilin), FAN Yunjie, WANG Liping, WEN Lirong,
ZHAO Lihong, LIU Ying, LIU Ailing (58' QIU Haiyan), BAI Jie, SUN Wen, JIN Yan (51'
ZHANG Ouying). (Coach: YUANAN Ma).
Ghana: Memunatu SULEMANA, Patience SACKEY *(YC28)*, Elizabeth BAIDU, Rita
YEBOAH *(YC16)*, Regina ANSAH, Adjoa BAYOR (56' Lydia ANKRAH), Genevive
CLOTTEY, Stella QUARTEY, Alberta SACKEY, Nana GYAMFUAH (74' Mavis
DGAJMAH), Vivian MENSAH. (Coach: Emmanuel AFRANI).
Goals: 9' SUN Wen 1-0, 16' JIN Yan 2-0, 21', 54' SUN Wen 3-0, 4-0, 82',
90+1' ZHANG Ouying 5-0, 6-0, 90+2' ZHAO Lihong 7-0.
Referee: Elke GÜNTHER (Germany)   Attendance: 17.668

26.06.1999   Giants Stadium, East Rutherford: China PR – Australia 3-1 (1-0)
China PR: GAO Hong, PU Wei, FAN Yunjie *(YC4)*, WANG Liping, WEN Lirong *(YC70)*,
ZHAO Lihong (75' XIE Huilin), LIU Ying, LIU Ailing, BAI Jie, SUN Wen (63' QIU Haiyan),
JIN Yan (46' ZHANG Ouying). (Coach: YUANAN Ma).
Australia: Bellinda KITCHING, Dianne ALAGICH, Cheryl SALISBURY (86' Peita-Claire
HEPPERLIN), Bridgette STARR, Traci BARTLETT, Anissa TANN DARBY, Alicia
FERGUSON, Kelly GOLEBIOWSKI, Lisa CASAGRANDE (72' Angela IANNOTTA),
Alison FORMAN, Julie MURRAY. (Coach: Greg BROWN).
Goals: 39', 51' SUN Wen 1-0, 2-0, 66' Cheryl SALISBURY 2-1, 73' LIU Ying 3-1.
Referee: Sandra HUNT (United States)   Attendance: 29.401

Sent-off: 2' Alicia FERGUSON.

26.06.1999   Soldier Field, Chicago: Ghana – Sweden 0-2 (0-0)
Ghana: Memunatu SULEMANA, Lydia ANKRAH (65' Sheila OKAI *(YC81)*), Patience
SACKEY, Elizabeth BAIDU, Adjoa BAYOR, Genevive CLOTTEY, Barikisu TETTEY
QUAO, Stella QUARTEY, Alberta SACKEY, Vivian MENSAH, Nana GYAMFUAH *(YC10)*
(84' Mercy TAGOE). (Coach: Emmanuel AFRANI).
Sweden: Ulrika KARLSSON, Karolina WESTBERG, Jane TÖRNQVIST, Gärd Kristin
BENGTSSON (60' Tina NORDLUND), Åsa LÖNNQVIST, Cecilia SANDELL, Malin Sofi
MOSTRÖM, Malin Elisabeth ANDERSSON, Hanna Carolina LJUNGBERG (6' Therese
LUNDIN), Victoria Margareta Sandell SVENSSON, Malin GUSTAFSSON (87' Linda
FAGERSTRÖM). (Coach: Marika Susan DOMANSKI LYFORS).
Goals: 58', 86' Victoria Margareta Sandell SVENSSON 0-1, 0-2.
Referee: Sonia DENONCOURT (Canada)   Attendance: 34.256

Team	Pld	W	D	L	GF	GA	GD	Pts
China PR	3	3	0	0	12	2	10	9
Sweden	3	2	0	1	6	3	3	6
Australia	3	0	1	2	3	7	-4	1
Ghana	3	0	1	2	1	10	-9	1

QUARTER-FINALS

30.06.1999   Spartan Stadium, San Jose: China PR – Russia 2-0 (1-0)
China PR: GAO Hong, PU Wei (80' QIU Haiyan *(YC90+2)*), FAN Yunjie, WANG Liping,
WEN Lirong, ZHAO Lihong, LIU Ying, LIU Ailing, BAI Jie, SUN Wen, JIN Yan (89'
ZHANG Ouying). (Coach: YUANAN Ma).
Russia: Svetlana PETKO, Marina BURAKOVA, Natalia FILIPPOVA, Tatiana CHEVERDA
(YC35), Natalia BARBASHINA (68' Larissa SAVINA), Natalia KARASEVA, Galina
KOMAROVA (88' Alexandra SVETLITSKAYA), Tatiana EGOROVA (46' Elena FOMINA),
Olga KARASSEVA, Irina GRIGORIEVA, Olga LETYUSHOVA. (Coach: Yuri
BYSTRITSKIY).
Goals: 37' PU Wei 1-0, 56' JIN Yan 2-0.
Referee: Nicole PETIGNAT (Switzerland)   Attendance: 21.411

30.06.1999   Spartan Stadium, San Jose: Norway – Sweden 3-1 (0-0)
Norway: Bente NORDBY, Brit SANDAUNE, Gøril KRINGEN, Linda MEDALEN, Unni
LEHN (77' Dagny MELLGREN), Hege RIISE, Monica KNUDSEN, Silje JØRGENSEN,
Tone Gunn FRUSTØL (46' Solveig GULBRANDSEN *(YC55)*), Ann Kristin AARØNES (81'
Anita RAPP), Marianne PETTERSEN. (Coach: Per-Mathias HØGMO).
Sweden: Ulrika KARLSSON, Karolina WESTBERG, Jane TÖRNQVIST, Gärd Kristin
BENGTSSON (46' Therese LUNDIN), Åsa LÖNNQVIST, Cecilia SANDELL, Malin Sofi
MOSTRÖM, Malin Elisabeth ANDERSSON, Tina NORDLUND (81' Minna HEPONIEMI),
Victoria Margareta Sandell SVENSSON, Malin GUSTAFSSON (72' Jessika SUNDH).
(Coach: Marika Susan DOMANSKI LYFORS).
Goals: 51' Ann Kristin AARØNES 1-0, 58' Marianne PETTERSEN 2-0,
72' Hege RIISE 3-0 (p), 90+1' Malin Sofi MOSTRÖM 3-1.
Referee: IM Eun-Ju (Korea Republic)   Attendance: 21.411

01.07.1999   FedEx Field, Landover: United States – Germany 3-2 (1-2)
United States: Briana Collette SCURRY, Kathryn Michele MARKGRAF Sobrero, Joy Lynn
FAWCETT Biefeld, Carla Werden OVERBECK, Kristine Marie LILLY Heavey, Brandi
Denise CHASTAIN (73' Lorraine Ming (Lorrie) FAIR), Julie Maurine FOUDY (65' Shannon
Ann MACMILLAN), Michelle Anne AKERS, Tiffeny Carleen MILBRETT, Mariel Margaret
(Mia) HAMM, Cynthia Marie (Cindy) PARLOW Cone (85' Tiffany Marie ROBERTS
Sahaydak). (Coach: Tony DiCICCO).
Germany: Silke ROTTENBERG, Sandra MINNERT, Doris FITSCHEN *(YC53)*, Ariane
HINGST, Stephanie JONES, Pia WUNDERLICH (53' Monika MEYER), Maren MEINERT,
Bettina WIEGMANN, Birgit PRINZ, Inka GRINGS (90+2' Melanie HOFFMANN), Sandra
SMISEK (84' Renate LINGOR). (Coach: Tina THEUNE).
Goals: 5' Brandi Denise CHASTAIN 0-1 (og), 16' Tiffeny Carleen MILBRETT 1-1,
45+1' Bettina WIEGMANN 1-2, 49' Brandi Denise CHASTAIN 2-2,
66' Joy Lynn FAWCETT Biefeld 3-2.
Referee: Martha TORO (Colombia)   Attendance: 54.642

34

01.07.1999   FedEx Field, Landover: Brazil – Nigeria 4-3 (3-0, 3-3) **(AET)**
Brazil: Marlisa Wahlbrink "MARAVILHA", TÂNIA Maria Pereira Ribeiro, Alissandra
Cavalcante "NENÊ", ELANE dos Santos Rego, SUZANA Ferreira da Silva *(YC81)*, Miraildes
Maciel Mota "FORMIGA", Sisleide do Amor Lima "SISSI", Maria Dias Aparecida de Souza
"CIDINHA", RAQUEL de Souza Noronha (66' ANDRÉIA dos Santos), Delma Gonçalves
"PRETINHA", KÁTIA Cilene Teixeira da Silva. (Coach: WILSON DE OLIVEIRA Riça).
Nigeria: Ann CHIEJINE (40' Judith CHIME), Yinka KUDAISI (77' Adanna NWANERI
(YC102)), Florence OMAGBEMI *(YC28)*, Eberechi OPARA, Prisca EMEAFU, Nkiru
OKOSIEME, Patience AVRE *(RC87)*, Ifeanyi CHIEJINE (26' Florence Kikelomo AJAYI),
Mercy AKIDE, Nkechi EGBE, Rita NWADIKE *(YC12)*. (Coach: Mabo ISMAILA).
Goals: 4', 22' Maria Dias Aparecida de Souza "CIDINHA" 1-0, 2-0, 35' Alissandra Cavalcante
"NENÊ" 3-0, 63' Prisca EMEAFU 3-1, 72' Nkiru OKOSIEME 3-2, 85' Nkechi EGBE 3-3,
104' Sisleide do Amor Lima "SISSI" 4-3.
Referee: Virginia TOVAR Dias (Mexico)   Attendance: 54.642

Sent-off: 87' Patience AVRE.

SEMI-FINALS

04.07.1999   Stanford Stadium, Stanford: United States – Brazil 2-0 (1-0)
United States: Briana Collette SCURRY, Kathryn Michele MARKGRAF Sobrero, Joy Lynn
FAWCETT Biefeld, Carla Werden OVERBECK, Kristine Marie LILLY Heavey, Brandi
Denise CHASTAIN, Julie Maurine FOUDY, Michelle Anne AKERS *(YC90)*, Tiffeny Carleen
MILBRETT (88' Danielle Ruth Garrett FOTOPOULOS), Mariel Margaret (Mia) HAMM (85'
Lorraine Ming (Lorrie) FAIR), Cynthia Marie (Cindy) PARLOW Cone (62' Shannon Ann
MACMILLAN). (Coach: Tony DiCICCO).
Brazil: Marlisa Wahlbrink "MARAVILHA", TÂNIA Maria Pereira Ribeiro *(YC13)*, JULIANA
Ribeiro Cabral, Alissandra Cavalcante "NENÊ", ELANE dos Santos Rego, SUZANA Ferreira
da Silva (70' ANDRÉIA dos Santos), Miraildes Maciel Mota "FORMIGA", Sisleide do Amor
Lima "SISSI" *(YC41)*, Maria Dias Aparecida de Souza "CIDINHA", Delma Gonçalves
"PRETINHA", KÁTIA Cilene Teixeira da Silva *(YC90+2)*. (Coach: WILSON DE OLIVEIRA
Riça).
Goals: 5' Cynthia Marie (Cindy) PARLOW Cone 1-0, 80' Michelle Anne AKERS 2-0 (p).
Referee: Katriina ELOVIRTA (Finland)   Attendance: 73.123

05.07.1999   Foxboro Stadium, Foxborough: Norway – China PR 0-5 (0-2)
Norway: Bente NORDBY, Brit SANDAUNE, Gøril KRINGEN, Linda MEDALEN, Solveig
GULBRANDSEN, Unni LEHN (46' Dagny MELLGREN), Hege RIISE, Monica KNUDSEN
(76' Tone Gunn FRUSTØL), Silje JØRGENSEN, Ann Kristin AARØNES (46' Ragnhild Øren
GULBRANDSEN), Marianne PETTERSEN. (Coach: Per-Mathias HØGMO).
China PR: GAO Hong, PU Wei (76' ZHANG Ouying), FAN Yunjie, WANG Liping, WEN
Lirong, ZHAO Lihong (78' QIU Haiyan), LIU Ying, LIU Ailing, BAI Jie, SUN Wen, JIN
Yan. (Coach: YUANAN Ma).
Goals: 3' SUN Wen 0-1, 14', 51' LIU Ailing 0-2, 0-3, 65' FAN Yunjie 0-4,
72' SUN Wen 0-5 (p).
Referee: Sonia DENONCOURT (Canada)   Attendance: 8.986

THIRD PLACE MATCH

10.07.1999   Rose Bowl, Pasadena: Brazil – Norway 0-0
Brazil: Marlisa Wahlbrink "MARAVILHA", TÂNIA Maria Pereira Ribeiro *(YC55)*, JULIANA
Ribeiro Cabral, Alissandra Cavalcante "NENÊ", ELANE dos Santos Rego, SUZANA Ferreira
da Silva (72' ANDRÉIA dos Santos), Miraildes Maciel Mota "FORMIGA", Sisleide do Amor
Lima "SISSI", Maria Dias Aparecida de Souza "CIDINHA", Delma Gonçalves "PRETINHA",
KÁTIA Cilene Teixeira da Silva. (Coach: WILSON DE OLIVEIRA Riça).
Norway: Bente NORDBY, Brit SANDAUNE, Gøril KRINGEN, Henriette VIKER, Linda
MEDALEN, Solveig GULBRANDSEN, Hege RIISE, Monica KNUDSEN, Silje
JØRGENSEN, Ragnhild Øren GULBRANDSEN (62' Ann Kristin AARØNES), Marianne
PETTERSEN (58' Dagny MELLGREN). (Coach: Per-Mathias HØGMO).
Referee: IM Eun-Ju (Korea Republic)   Attendance: 90.185

Penalties: Hege RIISE 0-1, Delma Gonçalves "PRETINHA" missed, Marianne
PETTERSEN 0-2, Maria Dias Aparecida de Souza "CIDINHA" 1-2, Silje
JØRGENSEN missed, KÁTIA Cilene Teixeira da Silva 2-2, Brit SANDAUNE 2-3,
ANDRÉIA dos Santos 3-3, Solveig GULBRANDSEN 3-4, Alissandra Cavalcante
"NENÊ" 4-4, Ann Kristin AARØNES missed, Miraildes Maciel Mota "FORMIGA"
5-4.

After extra time. Brazil won 5-4 on penalties.

FINAL

10.07.1999   Rose Bowl, Pasadena: United States – China PR 0-0
United States: Briana Collette SCURRY, Kathryn Michele MARKGRAF Sobrero, Joy Lynn
FAWCETT Biefeld, Carla Werden OVERBECK, Kristine Marie LILLY Heavey, Brandi
Denise CHASTAIN, Julie Maurine FOUDY, Michelle Anne AKERS *(YC74)* (91' Sara Eve
WHALEN Hess), Tiffeny Carleen MILBRETT (115' Tisha Lea VENTURINI Hoch), Mariel
Margaret (Mia) HAMM, Cynthia Marie (Cindy) PARLOW Cone (57' Shannon Ann
MACMILLAN). (Coach: Tony DiCICCO).
China PR: GAO Hong, PU Wei (59' ZHANG Ouying *(YC70))*, FAN Yunjie, WANG Liping,
WEN Lirong, ZHAO Lihong (114' QIU Haiyan), LIU Ying, LIU Ailing *(YC80)*, BAI Jie, SUN
Wen, JIN Yan (119' XIE Huilin). (Coach: YUANAN Ma).
Referee: Nicole PETIGNAT (Switzerland)   Attendance: 90.185

Penalties: XIE Huilin 0-1, Carla Werden OVERBECK 1-1, QIU Haiyan 1-2, Cynthia
Marie (Cindy) PARLOW Cone 2-2, LIU Ying missed, Kristine Marie LILLY Heavey
3-2, ZHANG Ouying 3-3, Mariel Margaret (Mia) HAMM 4-3, SUN Wen 4-4, Brandi
Denise CHASTAIN 5-4.

After extra time. The United States won 5-4 on penalties.

The United States won the World Cup.

FIFA WOMEN'S WORLD CUP – USA 2003

GROUP STAGE

GROUP A

20.09.2003   Lincoln Financial Field, Philadelphia: Negeria – Korea DPR 0-3 (0-1)
Nigeria: Predious Uzoaru DEDE, Bunmi KAYODE, Florence Kikelomo AJAYI *(YC28)*,
Florence IWETA, Florence OMAGBEMI (44' Maureen MMADU), Efioanwan EKPO,
Perpetua Ijeoma NKWOCHA, Stella MBACHU, Ifeanyi CHIEJINE (85' Onome EBI), Mercy
AKIDE *(YC22)*, Nkechi EGBE (46' Patience AVRE). (Coach: Samuel OKPODU).
Korea DPR: RI Jong-Hui, YUN In-Sil, RA Mi-Ae, JANG Ok-Gyong, JON Hye-Yong *(YC71)*,
RI Un-Gyong, YUN Yong-Hui (57' PAK Kyong-Sun), O Kum-Ran, RI Hyang-Ok *(YC25)*, RI
Kum-Suk (81' HO Sun-Hui), JIN Pyol-Hui. (Coach: RI Song-Gun).
Goals: 13' JIN Pyol-Hui 0-1, 73' RI Un-Gyong 0-2, 88' JIN Pyol-Hui 0-3.
Referee: Nicole PETIGNAT (Switzerland)   Attendance: 24.346

21.09.2003   Robert F. Kennedy Memorial Stadium, Washington:
        United States – Sweden 3-1 (2-0)
United States: Briana Collette SCURRY *(YC13)*, Christie PEARCE, Kathryn Michele
MARKGRAF Sobrero, Joy Lynn FAWCETT Biefeld, Shannon BOXX, Kristine Marie LILLY
Heavey, Brandi Denise CHASTAIN (46' Catherine WHITEHILL), Julie Maurine FOUDY,
Abby WAMBACH (56' Tiffeny Carleen MILBRETT), Mariel Margaret (Mia) HAMM,
Cynthia Marie (Cindy) PARLOW Cone (70' Alyson Kay (Aly) WAGNER *(YC72)*). (Coach:
April HEINRICHS).
Sweden: Caroline JÖNSSON, Karolina WESTBERG, Jane TÖRNQVIST, Sara LARSSON,
Hanna Gunilla MARKLUND, Kerstin Ingrid Therese SJÖGRAN (46' Frida Christina
ÖSTBERG), Linda FAGERSTRÖM, Malin Sofi MOSTRÖM, Malin Elisabeth ANDERSSON
(77' Anna SJÖSTRÖM *(YC90+3)*), Hanna Carolina LJUNGBERG (83' Josefine ÖQVIST),
Victoria Margareta Sandell SVENSSON. (Coach: Marika Susan DOMANSKI LYFORS).
Goals: 27' Kristine Marie LILLY Heavey 1-0, 36' Cynthia Marie (Cindy) PARLOW Cone 2-0,
58' Victoria Margareta Sandell SVENSSON 2-1, 78' Shannon BOXX 3-1.
Referee: ZHANG Dongqing (China PR)   Attendance: 34.144

25.09.2003   Lincoln Financial Field, Philadelphia: Sweden – Korea DPR 1-0 (1-0)
Sweden: Caroline JÖNSSON, Karolina WESTBERG *(YC52)*, Jane TÖRNQVIST, Sara
LARSSON, Hanna Gunilla MARKLUND, Frida Christina ÖSTBERG, Linda FAGERSTRÖM
(56' Anna SJÖSTRÖM), Malin Sofi MOSTRÖM, Malin Elisabeth ANDERSSON (65' Gärd
Kristin BENGTSSON), Hanna Carolina LJUNGBERG (86' Josefine ÖQVIST), Victoria
Margareta Sandell SVENSSON. (Coach: Marika Susan DOMANSKI LYFORS).
Korea DPR: RI Jong-Hui, SIN Kum-Ok (55' YUN In-Sil), RA Mi-Ae (62' SONG Jong-Sun),
JANG Ok-Gyong *(YC56)*, JON Hye-Yong, RI Un-Gyong, YUN Yong-Hui (36' HO Sun-Hui),
O Kum-Ran, RI Hyang-Ok, RI Kum-Suk, JIN Pyol-Hui. (Coach: RI Song-Gun).
Goal: 7' Victoria Margareta Sandell SVENSSON 1-0.
Referee: Tammy Nicole OGSTON (Australia)   Attendance: 31.553

25.09.2003   Lincoln Financial Field, Philadelphia: United States – Nigeria 5-0 (2-0)
United States: Briana Collette SCURRY, Catherine WHITEHILL, Kathryn Michele
MARKGRAF Sobrero, Kylie Elizabeth BIVENS, Joy Lynn FAWCETT Biefeld, Shannon
BOXX (71' Tiffany Marie ROBERTS Sahaydak), Alyson Kay (Aly) WAGNER (46' Abby
WAMBACH), Kristine Marie LILLY Heavey, Julie Maurine FOUDY, Mariel Margaret (Mia)
HAMM, Cynthia Marie (Cindy) PARLOW Cone (57' Tiffeny Carleen MILBRETT). (Coach:
April HEINRICHS).
Nigeria: Predious Uzoaru DEDE, Bunmi KAYODE, Florence Kikelomo AJAYI, Florence
OMAGBEMI (YC76), Maureen MMADU, Nkiru OKOSIEME, Patience AVRE, Perpetua
Ijeoma NKWOCHA, Stella MBACHU, Ifeanyi CHIEJINE, Mercy AKIDE. (Coach: Samuel
OKPODU).
Goals: 6', 12' Mariel Margaret (Mia) HAMM 1-0 (p), 2-0, 47' Cynthia Marie (Cindy)
PARLOW Cone 3-0, 65' Abby WAMBACH 4-0, 89' Julie Maurine FOUDY 5-0 (p).
Referee: Florencia ROMANO (Argentina)   Attendance: 31.553

28.09.1999   MAPFRE Stadium, Columbus: Sweden – Nigeria 3-0 (0-0)
Sweden: Caroline JÖNSSON, Karolina WESTBERG, Gärd Kristin BENGTSSON (46' Anna
SJÖSTRÖM), Sara LARSSON, Hanna Gunilla MARKLUND, Sara CALL, Frida Christina
ÖSTBERG, Malin Sofi MOSTRÖM, Malin Elisabeth ANDERSSON (66' Kerstin Ingrid
Therese SJÖGRAN), Hanna Carolina LJUNGBERG, Victoria Margareta Sandell SVENSSON
(85' Josefine ÖQVIST). (Coach: Marika Susan DOMANSKI LYFORS).
Nigeria: Predious Uzoaru DEDE, Florence Kikelomo AJAYI, Florence IWETA (83' Onome
EBI), Florence OMAGBEMI, Maureen MMADU, Nkiru OKOSIEME (65' Efioanwan EKPO),
Patience AVRE (89' Olaitan YUSUF), Perpetua Ijeoma NKWOCHA, Stella MBACHU,
Ifeanyi CHIEJINE, Mercy AKIDE. (Coach: Samuel OKPODU).
Goals: 56', 79' Hanna Carolina LJUNGBERG 1-0, 2-0, 81' Malin Sofi MOSTRÖM 3-0.
Referee: Sonia DENONCOURT (Canada)   Attendance: 22.828

28.09.2003   MAPFRE Stadium, Columbus: Korea DPR – United States 0-3 (0-1)
Korea DPR: RI Jong-Hui, YUN In-Sil, SIN Kum-Ok (26' JON Hye-Yong), RA Mi-Ae, JANG
Ok-Gyong, RI Un-Gyong, YUN Yong-Hui (74' PAK Kyong-Sun (YC90+1)), O Kum-Ran
(YC16) (53' SONG Jong-Sun), RI Hyang-Ok, RI Kum-Suk, JIN Pyol-Hui. (Coach: RI Song-
Gun).
United States: Briana Collette SCURRY, Christie PEARCE, Catherine WHITEHILL, Kathryn
Michele MARKGRAF Sobrero (73' Danielle SLATON), Kylie Elizabeth BIVENS, Joy Lynn
FAWCETT Biefeld, Alyson Kay (Aly) WAGNER, Kristine Marie LILLY Heavey (46' Julie
Maurine FOUDY), Tiffany Marie ROBERTS Sahaydak, Tiffeny Carleen MILBRETT (YC40),
Abby WAMBACH (YC22) (56' Shannon Ann MACMILLAN). (Coach: April HEINRICHS).
Goals: 17' Abby WAMBACH 0-1 (p), 48', 66' Catherine WHITEHILL 0-2, 0-3.
Referee: SUELI Terezinha TORTURA (Brazil)   Attendance: 22.828

Team	Pld	W	D	L	GF	GA	GD	Pts
United States	*3*	*3*	*0*	*0*	*11*	*1*	*10*	*9*
Sweden	*3*	*2*	*0*	*1*	*5*	*3*	*2*	*6*
Korea DPR	3	1	0	2	3	4	-1	3
Nigeria	3	0	0	3	0	11	-11	0

GROUP B

20.09.2003 Lincoln Financial Field, Philidelphia: Norway – France 2-0 (0-0)
Norway: Bente NORDBY, Ane STANGELAND Horpestad, Gunhild Bentzen FØLSTAD, Brit
SANDAUNE, Solveig GULBRANDSEN (80' Trine RØNNING), Unni LEHN (89' Hege
RIISE), Monica KNUDSEN, Lise KLAVENESS (YC90+1), Marianne PETTERSEN (90+1'
Linda ØRMEN), Anita RAPP (YC86), Dagny MELLGREN. (Coach: Åge STEEN).
France: Corinne DIACRE, Celine MARTY, Laura GEORGES, Sonia BOMPASTOR, Sabrina
Marie-Christine VIGUIER, Peggy PROVOST, Sandrine SOUBEYRAND, Élodie WOOCK,
Stéphanie MUGNERET-BÉGHÉ (82' Marie-Ange KRAMO), Hoda LATTAF (72' Laëtitia
Françoise Andree (Toto) TONAZZI), Marinette PICHON. (Coaches: Corinne DIACRE &
Élisabeth LOISEL).
Goals: 47' Anita RAPP 1-0, 66' Dagny MELLGREN 2-0.
Referee: Kari SEITZ (United States) Attendance: 24.346

21.09.2003 Robert F. Kennedy Memorial Stadium, Washington:
        Brazil – Korea Republic 3-0 (1-0)
Brazil: ANDRÉIA Suntaque, TÂNIA Maria Pereira Ribeiro, Renata Aparecida da Costa
"KÓKI", JULIANA Ribeiro Cabral, ROSANA dos Santos Augusto, Miraildes Maciel Mota
"FORMIGA" (YC2) (89' PRISCILA Faria de Oliveira), SIMONE Gomes Jatobá, DANIELA
Alves Lima, ANDRÉIA dos Santos (78' CRISTIANE Rozeira de Souza Silva), MARTA
Vieira da Silva, KÁTIA Cilene Teixeira da Silva. (Coach: PAULO GONÇALVES).
Korea Republic: KIM Jung-Mi, KIM Yu-Mi (YC22) (46' JIN Suk-Hee (YC71)), SONG Ju-
Hee, SHIN Sun-Nam, KIM Yu-Jin, YOO Young-Sil, KIM Kyul-Sil (65' HWANG Insun),
KIM Jin-Hee (49' SUNG Hyun-Ah), HAN Jin-Sook, PARK Eun-Sun, LEE Ji-Eun. (Coach:
AN Jong-Goan).
Goals: 14' MARTA Vieira da Silva 1-0 (p), 55', 62' KÁTIA Cilene Teixeira da Silva 2-0, 3-0.
Referee: Tammy Nicole OGSTON (Australia) Attendance: 34.144

24.09.2003   Robert F. Kennedy Memorial Stadium, Washington:
    Norway – Brazil 1-4 (1-2)
Norway: Bente NORDBY, Ane STANGELAND Horpestad, Trine RØNNING (YC77),
Gunhild Bentzen FØLSTAD, Brit SANDAUNE, Solveig GULBRANDSEN (74' Lise
KLAVENESS), Unni LEHN (74' Hege RIISE), Monica KNUDSEN, Marianne PETTERSEN,
Anita RAPP (46' Linda ØRMEN), Dagny MELLGREN. (Coach: Åge STEEN).
Brazil: ANDRÉIA Suntaque, TÂNIA Maria Pereira Ribeiro, Renata Aparecida da Costa
"KÓKI" (YC51), JULIANA Ribeiro Cabral, ROSANA dos Santos Augusto, Miraildes Maciel
Mota "FORMIGA" (88' RAFAELA Andrade de Moraes), SIMONE Gomes Jatobá, DANIELA
Alves Lima (90' PRISCILA Faria de Oliveira), ANDRÉIA dos Santos (80' CRISTIANE
Rozeira de Souza Silva), MARTA Vieira da Silva, KÁTIA Cilene Teixeira da Silva. (Coach:
PAULO GONÇALVES).
Goals: 26' DANIELA Alves Lima 0-1, 37' ROSANA dos Santos Augusto 0-2, 45' Marianne
PETTERSEN 1-2, 59' MARTA Vieira da Silva 1-3, 68' KÁTIA Cilene Teixeira da Silva 1-4.
Referee: Xonam AGBOYI (Togo)   Attendance: 16.316

24.09.2003   Robert F. Kennedy Memorial Stadium, Washington:
    France – Korea Republic 1-0 (0-0)
France: Corinne DIACRE (YC65), Celine MARTY, Laura GEORGES, Sonia BOMPASTOR,
Anne-Laure CASSELEUX (81' Emmanuelle SYKORA), Peggy PROVOST, Sandrine
SOUBEYRAND, Marie-Ange KRAMO, Élodie WOOCK (YC37) (89' Virginie DESSALLE),
Stéphanie MUGNERET-BÉGHÉ (68' Laëtitia Françoise Andree (Toto) TONAZZI), Marinette
PICHON. (Coaches: Corinne DIACRE & Élisabeth LOISEL).
Korea Republic: KIM Jung-Mi, KIM Yu-Mi, SHIN Sun-Nam (85' KIM Ju-
Hee), KIM Yu-Jin, YOO Young-Sil (YC45) (83' JIN Suk-Hee), KIM Kyul-Sil (75' LEE
Myung-Hwa (YC83)), KIM Jin-Hee, HAN Jin-Sook, PARK Eun-Sun, LEE Ji-Eun. (Coach:
AN Jong-Goan).
Goal: 84' Marinette PICHON 1-0.
Referee: ZHANG Dongqing (China PR)   Attendance: 16.316

27.09.2003   Gilette Stadium, Foxborough: Korea Republic – Norway 1-7 (0-4)
Korea Republic: KIM Jung-Mi, KIM Yu-Mi, SONG Ju-Hee, KIM Yu-Jin (55' JIN Suk-Hee),
YOO Young-Sil, KIM Ju-Hee, KIM Kyul-Sil, KIM Jin-Hee, HAN Jin-Sook (30' KIM Yoo-
Jin), PARK Eun-Sun (59' HONG Kyung-Suk), LEE Ji-Eun. (Coach: AN Jong-Goan).
Norway: Bente NORDBY, Marit Helene Fiane GRØDUM CHRISTENSEN, Ane
STANGELAND Horpestad, Trine RØNNING (69' Linda ØRMEN), Brit SANDAUNE,
Solveig GULBRANDSEN (73' Ingrid Camilla Fosse SÆTHRE), Unni LEHN, Monica
KNUDSEN, Lise KLAVENESS (81' Hege RIISE), Marianne PETTERSEN, Dagny
MELLGREN. (Coach: Åge STEEN).
Goals: 5' Solveig GULBRANDSEN 0-1, 24', 31' Dagny MELLGREN 0-2, 0-3,
40' Marianne PETTERSEN 0-4, 52' Brit SANDAUNE 0-5, 75' KIM Jin-Hee 1-5,
80', 90' Linda ØRMEN 1-6, 1-7.
Referee: Tammy Nicole OGSTON (Australia)   Attendance: 14.356

41

27.09.2003   Robert F. Kennedy Memorial Stadium, Washington:
    France – Brazil 1-1 (0-0)
France: Corinne DIACRE, Celine MARTY, Laura GEORGES, Sonia BOMPASTOR, Sabrina
Marie-Christine VIGUIER (85' Hoda LATTAF), Peggy PROVOST *(YC72)*, Sandrine
SOUBEYRAND, Marie-Ange KRAMO, Élodie WOOCK (73' Amelie COQUET), Stéphanie
MUGNERET-BÉGHÉ (46' Laëtitia Françoise Andree (Toto) TONAZZI), Marinette PICHON.
(Coaches: Corinne DIACRE & Élisabeth LOISEL).
Brazil: ANDRÉIA Suntaque, TÂNIA Maria Pereira Ribeiro (88' MÔNICA Angélica de
Paula), JULIANA Ribeiro Cabral, ROSANA dos Santos Augusto, SIMONE Gomes Jatobá,
DANIELA Alves Lima *(YC51)*, ANDRÉIA dos Santos, RAFAELA Andrade de Moraes,
PRISCILA Faria de Oliveira (46' CRISTIANE Rozeira de Souza Silva), MARTA Vieira da
Silva, KÁTIA Cilene Teixeira da Silva. (Coach: PAULO GONÇALVES).
Goals: 58' KÁTIA Cilene Teixeira da Silva 0-1, 90+2' Marinette PICHON 1-1.
Referee: Floarea Cristina Ionescu BABADAC (Romania)   Attendance: 17.618

Team	Pld	W	D	L	GF	GA	GD	Pts
Brazil	*3*	*2*	*1*	*0*	*8*	*2*	*6*	*7*
Norway	*3*	*2*	*0*	*1*	*10*	*5*	*5*	*6*
France	3	1	1	1	2	3	-1	4
Korea Republic	3	0	0	3	1	11	-10	0

GROUP C

20.09.2003   MAPFRE Stadium, Columbus: Germany – Canada 4-1 (1-1)
Germany: Silke ROTTENBERG, Kerstin STEGEMANN, Sandra MINNERT, Stefanie
GOTTSCHLICH, Ariane HINGST (65' Nia Tsholofelo KÜNZER), Renate LINGOR (73'
Kerstin GAREFREKES), Linda BRESONIK *(YC45+1)*, Stephanie JONES, Maren MEINERT
(YC78), Bettina WIEGMANN, Birgit PRINZ. (Coach: Tina THEUNE).
Canada: Karina LEBLANC *(YC21)*, Kristina KISS, Tanya DENNIS, Sharolta Louisa NONEN,
Charmaine HOOPER *(YC38)*, Andrea NEIL, Diana MATHESON, Brittany TIMKO, Christine
SINCLAIR, Kara Elise LANG (46' Rhian WILKINSON), Cristine LATHAM. (Coach: Even
Jostein PELLERUD).
Goals: 4' Christine SINCLAIR 0-1, 39' Bettina WIEGMANN 1-1 (p),
47' Stefanie GOTTSCHLICH 2-1, 75' Birgit PRINZ 3-1, 90+2' Kerstin GAREFREKES 4-1.
Referee: IM Eun-Ju (Korea Republic)   Attendance: 16.409

20.09.2003   MAPFRE Stadium, Columbus: Japan – Argentina 6-0 (2-0)
Japan: Nozomi YAMAGO, Kyoko YANO, Yumi OBE, Yasuyo YAMAGISHI (73' Hiromi
ISOZAKI), Tomomi MIYAMOTO, Tomoe KATO Sakai, Homare SAWA (80' Karina
MARUYAMA), Emi YAMAMOTO, Yayoi KOBAYASHI (57' Eriko ARAKAWA), Naoko
KAWAKAMI, Mio OTANI. (Coach: Eiji UEDA).
Argentina: Romina FERRO, Sabrina BARBITTA *(YC59)*, Clarisa HUBER, Marisa GEREZ,
Mariela RICOTTI (76' Noelia LOPEZ), Andrea GONSEBATE, Rosana GÓMEZ *(YC18)* (46'
Valeria COTELO), Fabiana VALLEJOS, Mariela CORONEL, Natalia GATTI (RC39), Maria
VILLANUEVA *(YC16)* (46' Karina ALVARIZA). (Coach: José Carlos BORRELLO).
Goals: 13, 38' Homare SAWA 1-0, 2-0, 64' Emi YAMAMOTO 3-0,
72', 75', 80' Mio OTANI 4-0, 5-0, 6-0.
Referee: Katriina ELOVIRTA (Finland)   Attendance: 16.409

Sent-off: 39' Natalia GATTI.

24.09.2003   MAPFRE Stadium, Columbus: Germany – Japan 3-0 (2-0)
Germany: Silke ROTTENBERG, Kerstin STEGEMANN, Sandra MINNERT, Stefanie
GOTTSCHLICH (64' Sandra SMISEK), Ariane HINGST (72' Linda BRESONIK), Renate
LINGOR, Kerstin GAREFREKES, Stephanie JONES, Maren MEINERT, Bettina
WIEGMANN (78' Nia Tsholofelo KÜNZER *(YC80)*), Birgit PRINZ. (Coach: Tina THEUNE).
Japan: Nozomi YAMAGO, Kyoko YANO (60' Hiromi ISOZAKI), Yumi OBE, Yasuyo
YAMAGISHI, Tomomi MIYAMOTO, Tomoe KATO Sakai (56' Miyuki YANAGITA),
Homare SAWA, Emi YAMAMOTO, Yayoi KOBAYASHI (56' Eriko ARAKAWA), Naoko
KAWAKAMI, Mio OTANI. (Coach: Eiji UEDA).
Goals: 23' Sandra MINNERT 1-0, 36', 66' Birgit PRINZ 2-0, 3-0.
Referee: SUELI Terezinha TORTURA (Brazil)   Attendance: 15.529

24.09.1999   MAPFRE Stadium, Columbus: Canada – Argentina 3-0 (1-0)
Canada: Taryn SWIATEK, Kristina KISS, Tanya DENNIS, Rhian WILKINSON *(YC62)* (75'
Silvana BURTINI), Sharolta Louisa NONEN, Charmaine HOOPER, Diana MATHESON
(YC41), Brittany TIMKO, Christine SINCLAIR, Kara Elise LANG, Cristine LATHAM (83'
Sasha Ajua ANDREWS *(YC86)*). (Coach: Even Jostein PELLERUD).
Argentina: Romina FERRO, Sabrina BARBITTA, Clarisa HUBER, Marisa GEREZ, Mariela
RICOTTI *(YC29)* (78' Noelia LOPEZ), Andrea GONSEBATE, Rosana GÓMEZ, Fabiana
VALLEJOS, Mariela CORONEL (84' Yanina GAITAN), Marisol MEDINA, Maria
VILLANUEVA (75' Karina ALVARIZA). (Coach: José Carlos BORRELLO).
Goals: 19' Charmaine HOOPER 1-0 (p), 79', 82' Cristine LATHAM 2-0, 3-0.
Referee: Nicole PETIGNAT (Switzerland)   Attendance: 15.529

27.09.1999   Robert F. Kennedy Memorial Stadium, Washington:
Argentina – Germany 1-6 (0-4)
Argentina: Romina FERRO, Sabrina BARBITTA, Clarisa HUBER, Marisa GEREZ, Andrea
GONSEBATE, Noelia LOPEZ, Rosana GÓMEZ (56' Yanina GAITAN), Fabiana
VALLEJOS, Mariela CORONEL, Marisol MEDINA, Maria VILLANUEVA (85' Karina
ALVARIZA). (Coach: José Carlos BORRELLO).
Germany: Silke ROTTENBERG, Kerstin STEGEMANN, Sandra MINNERT, Stefanie
GOTTSCHLICH (46' Conny POHLERS), Ariane HINGST, Renate LINGOR, Kerstin
GAREFREKES (46' Martina MÜLLER), Stephanie JONES (62' Sonja Beate FUSS), Maren
MEINERT, Bettina WIEGMANN, Birgit PRINZ. (Coach: Tina THEUNE).
Goals: 3' Maren MEINERT 0-1, 24' Bettina WIEGMANN 0-2 (p), 32' Birgit PRINZ 0-3,
43' Maren MEINERT 0-4, 71' Yanina GAITAN 1-4, 89' Conny POHLERS 1-5,
90+2' Martina MÜLLER 1-6.
Referee: Bola ABIDOYE (Nigeria)   Attendance: 17.618

27.09.1999   Gillette Stadium, Foxborough: Canada – Japan 3-1 (1-1)
Canada: Taryn SWIATEK, Tanya DENNIS, Sharolta Louisa NONEN, Isabelle MORNEAU
(YC45+1), Charmaine HOOPER, Andrea NEIL (77' Kristina KISS), Diana MATHESON,
Brittany TIMKO, Christine SINCLAIR, Kara Elise LANG (85' Rhian WILKINSON), Cristine
LATHAM (60' Silvana BURTINI). (Coach: Even Jostein PELLERUD).
Japan: Nozomi YAMAGO, Hiromi ISOZAKI, Yumi OBE, Yasuyo YAMAGISHI, Tomomi
MIYAMOTO, Tomoe KATO Sakai (62' Miyuki YANAGITA), Homare SAWA, Emi
YAMAMOTO (89' Aya MIYAMA), Yayoi KOBAYASHI (54' Eriko ARAKAWA), Naoko
KAWAKAMI, Mio OTANI. (Coach: Eiji UEDA).
Goals: 20' Homare SAWA 0-1, 36', 49' Christine SINCLAIR 1-1, 2-1,
72' Kara Elise LANG 3-1.
Referee: IM Eun-Ju (Korea Republic)   Attendance: 14.356

Team	Pld	W	D	L	GF	GA	GD	Pts
Germany	3	3	0	0	13	2	11	9
Canada	3	2	0	1	7	5	2	6
Japan	3	1	0	2	7	6	1	3
Argentina	3	0	0	3	1	15	-14	0

GROUP D

20.09.2003 Stubhub Center, Carson: China PR – Ghana 1-0 (1-0)
China PR: ZHAO Yan, LI Jie, PU Wei, FAN Yunjie, WANG Liping, PAN Lina (36' QU
Feifei), ZHAO Lihong (88' REN Liping), LIU Ying, HAN Duan (59' LIU Yali), BAI Jie, SUN
Wen. (Coach: MA Liangxing).
Ghana: Memunatu SULEMANA, Mavis DANSO, Yaa AVOE (58' Belinda KANDA), Lydia
ANKRAH, Patience SACKEY, Elizabeth BAIDU, Florence OKOE, Adjoa BAYOR, Genevive
CLOTTEY, Alberta SACKEY (83' Myralyn OSEI AGYEMANG), Mavis DGAJMAH *(YC90)*
(90+2' Akua ANOKYEWAA). (Coach: Oko ARYEE).
Goal: 29' SUN Wen 1-0.
Referee: Sonia DENONCOURT (Canada)   Attendance: 15.239

21.09.2003 Stubhub Center, Carson: Australia – Russia 1-2 (1-1)
Australia: Cassandra KELL, Dianne ALAGICH, Cheryl SALISBURY, Rhian DAVIES, Sacha
WAINWRIGHT (46' Bryony DUUS), Heather GARRIOCK, Joanne PETERS, Danielle
SMALL, Tal KARP (90+1' April MANN), Gillian FORSTER, Kelly GOLEBIOWSKI.
(Coach: Adrian SANTRAC).
Russia: Alla VOLKOVA, Oksana SHMACHKOVA, Marina SAENKO, Tatiana ZAYTSEVA,
Marina BURAKOVA, Anastasia PUSTOVOITOVA (67' Vera STROUKOVA), Natalia
BARBASHINA, Elena FOMINA *(YC83)*, Galina KOMAROVA, Tatiana EGOROVA (68'
Tatiana SKOTNIKOVA), Olga LETYUSHOVA *(YC87)*. (Coach: Yuri BYSTRITSKIY).
Goals: 38' Kelly GOLEBIOWSKI 1-0, 39' Dianne ALAGICH 1-1 (og).
Referee: Bola ABIDOYE (Nigeria)   Attendance: 175.239

25.09.2003 Stubhub Center, Carson: Ghana – Russia 0-3 (0-1)
Ghana: Memunatu SULEMANA, Mavis DANSO, Yaa AVOE (58' Alberta SACKEY), Lydia
ANKRAH, Patience SACKEY (78' Belinda KANDA), Elizabeth BAIDU, Florence OKOE,
Adjoa BAYOR, Genevive CLOTTEY, Myralyn OSEI AGYEMANG (52' Akua
ANOKYEWAA), Mavis DGAJMAH. (Coach: Oko ARYEE).
Russia: Alla VOLKOVA, Marina SAENKO (74' Anastasia PUSTOVOITOVA), Elena
DENCHTCHIK (46' Alexandra SVETLITSKAYA), Tatiana ZAYTSEVA, Marina
BURAKOVA, Vera STROUKOVA, Natalia BARBASHINA, Elena FOMINA, Galina
KOMAROVA, Tatiana EGOROVA (59' Tatiana SKOTNIKOVA), Olga LETYUSHOVA.
(Coach: Yuri BYSTRITSKIY).
Goals: 36' Marina SAENKO 0-1, 54' Natalia BARBASHINA 0-2,
80' Olga LETYUSHOVA 0-3.
Referee: Kari SEITZ (United States)   Attendance: 13.929

45

25.09.2003 Stubhub Center, Carson: China PR – Australia 1-1 (0-1)
China PR: ZHAO Yan, LI Jie, PU Wei, LIU Yali, FAN Yunjie, WANG Liping, ZHAO Lihong (85' QU Feifei), LIU Ying *(YC55)*, ZHANG Ouying (74' REN Liping), BAI Jie (90' TENG Wei), SUN Wen. (Coach: MA Liangxing).
Australia: Cassandra KELL, Dianne ALAGICH *(YC89)*, Cheryl SALISBURY, Rhian DAVIES, Karla REUTER, Heather GARRIOCK, Joanne PETERS, Danielle SMALL (76' Bryony DUUS), Tal KARP, Gillian FORSTER, Kelly GOLEBIOWSKI *(YC90+1)*. (Coach: Adrian SANTRAC).
Goals: 28' Heather GARRIOCK 0-1, 46' BAI Jie 1-1.
Referee: Katriina ELOVIRTA (Finland) Attendance: 13.929

28.09.2003 Providence Park, Portland: Ghana – Australia 2-1 (2-0)
Ghana: Memunatu SULEMANA, Mavis DANSO (75' Yaa AVOE), Lydia ANKRAH *(YC59)*, Patience SACKEY, Elizabeth BAIDU, Florence OKOE, Adjoa BAYOR, Genevive CLOTTEY, Gloria FORIWA (67' Myralyn OSEI AGYEMANG, 90+1' Akua ANOKYEWAA), Alberta SACKEY, Mavis DGAJMAH. (Coach: Oko ARYEE).
Australia: Melissa BARBIERI HUDSON, Dianne ALAGICH, Cheryl SALISBURY, Rhian DAVIES, Karla REUTER (90' Pamela GRANT), Heather GARRIOCK *(YC52)*, Joanne PETERS, Danielle SMALL, Tal KARP (33' Bryony DUUS), Gillian FORSTER (43' April MANN), Kelly GOLEBIOWSKI. (Coach: Adrian SANTRAC).
Goals: 34', 39' Alberta SACKEY 1-0, 2-0, 61' Heather GARRIOCK 2-1.
Referee: Xonam AGBOYI (Togo) Attendance: 19.132

28.09.2003 Providence Park, Portland: China PR – Russia 1-0 (1-0)
China PR: HAN Wenxia, LI Jie, PU Wei, LIU Yali, FAN Yunjie, WANG Liping, BI Yan (55' QU Feifei), ZHAO Lihong (62' REN Liping), LIU Ying, BAI Jie, SUN Wen. (Coach: MA Liangxing).
Russia: Alla VOLKOVA, Marina SAENKO, Tatiana ZAYTSEVA, Marina BURAKOVA, Vera STROUKOVA, Natalia BARBASHINA, Elena FOMINA *(YC90)*, Galina KOMAROVA, Tatiana EGOROVA, Alexandra SVETLITSKAYA, Olga LETYUSHOVA (66' Tatiana SKOTNIKOVA). (Coach: Yuri BYSTRITSKIY).
Goal: 16' BAI Jie 1-0.
Referee: Florencia ROMANO (Argentina) Attendance: 19.132

Team	Pld	W	D	L	GF	GA	GD	Pts
China PR	*3*	*2*	*1*	*0*	*3*	*1*	*2*	*7*
Russia	*3*	*2*	*0*	*1*	*5*	*2*	*3*	*6*
Ghana	3	1	0	2	2	5	-3	3
Australia	3	0	1	2	3	5	-2	1

QUARTER-FINALS

01.10.2003   Gillette Stadium, Foxborough: Brazil – Sweden 1-2 (1-1)
Brazil: ANDRÉIA Suntaque, TÂNIA Maria Pereira Ribeiro, Renata Aparecida da Costa "KÓKI", JULIANA Ribeiro Cabral *(YC52)*, ROSANA dos Santos Augusto, Miraildes Maciel Mota "FORMIGA" (81' KELLY Christina Pereira da Silva), SIMONE Gomes Jatobá (58' CRISTIANE Rozeira de Souza Silva), DANIELA Alves Lima *(YC37)*, ANDRÉIA dos Santos, MARTA Vieira da Silva, KÁTIA Cilene Teixeira da Silva. (Coach: PAULO GONÇALVES).
Sweden: Sofia LUNDGREN *(YC43)*, Karolina WESTBERG, Jane TÖRNQVIST, Sara LARSSON (90' Sara CALL), Hanna Gunilla MARKLUND, Frida Christina ÖSTBERG, Malin Sofi MOSTRÖM, Malin Elisabeth ANDERSSON (72' Kerstin Ingrid Therese SJÖGRAN), Hanna Carolina LJUNGBERG, Victoria Margareta Sandell SVENSSON, Anna SJÖSTRÖM *(YC15)*. (Coach: Marika Susan DOMANSKI LYFORS).
Goals: 23' Victoria Margareta Sandell SVENSSON 0-1, 44' MARTA Vieira da Silva 1-1, 53' Malin Elisabeth ANDERSSON 1-2.
Referee: ZHANG Dongqing (China PR)   Attendance: 25.103

01.10.2003   Gillette Stadium, Foxborough: United States – Norway 1-0 (1-0)
United States: Briana Collette SCURRY, Christie PEARCE, Catherine WHITEHILL, Kathryn Michele MARKGRAF Sobrero, Joy Lynn FAWCETT Biefeld, Shannon BOXX, Kristine Marie LILLY Heavey, Julie Maurine FOUDY (81' Kylie Elizabeth BIVENS), Abby WAMBACH, Mariel Margaret (Mia) HAMM, Cynthia Marie (Cindy) PARLOW Cone (72' Tiffeny Carleen MILBRETT). (Coach: April HEINRICHS).
Norway: Bente NORDBY *(YC66)*, Marit Helene Fiane GRØDUM CHRISTENSEN (77' Linda ØRMEN), Ane STANGELAND Horpestad, Trine RØNNING (24' Anita RAPP), Brit SANDAUNE, Solveig GULBRANDSEN, Unni LEHN *(YC80)* (84' Hege RIISE *(YC86)*), Monica KNUDSEN, Lise KLAVENESS *(YC75)*, Marianne PETTERSEN, Dagny MELLGREN. (Coach: Åge STEEN).
Goal: 24' Abby WAMBACH 1-0.
Referee: Nicole PETIGNAT (Switzerland)   Attendance: 25.103

02.10.2003   Providence Park, Portland: Germany – Russia 7-1 (1-0)
Germany: Silke ROTTENBERG, Kerstin STEGEMANN, Sandra MINNERT, Stefanie GOTTSCHLICH, Ariane HINGST, Renate LINGOR (82' Viola ODEBRECHT), Kerstin GAREFREKES, Maren MEINERT, Bettina WIEGMANN (66' Nia Tsholofelo KÜNZER), Birgit PRINZ, Martina MÜLLER (57' Pia WUNDERLICH *(YC66)*). (Coach: Tina THEUNE).
Russia: Alla VOLKOVA, Marina SAENKO, Tatiana ZAYTSEVA, Marina BURAKOVA, Vera STROUKOVA, Natalia BARBASHINA, Tatiana SKOTNIKOVA, Galina KOMAROVA, Tatiana EGOROVA (75' Marina KOLOMIETS), Alexandra SVETLITSKAYA (34' Elena DENCHTCHIK), Olga LETYUSHOVA (46' Elena DANILOVA). (Coach: Yuri BYSTRITSKIY).
Goals: 25' Martina MÜLLER 1-0, 57' Sandra MINNERT 2-0, 60' Pia WUNDERLICH 3-0, 62' Kerstin GAREFREKES 4-0, 70' Elena DANILOVA 4-1, 80' Birgit PRINZ 5-1, 85' Kerstin GAREFREKES 6-1, 89' Birgit PRINZ 7-1.
Referee: IM Eun-Ju (Korea Republic)   Attendance: 20.012

02.10.2003   Providence Park, Portland: China PR – Canada 0-1 (0-1)
China PR: HAN Wenxia, LI Jie, PU Wei, LIU Yali (82' TENG Wei *(YC90+2)*), FAN Yunjie,
WANG Liping, BI Yan, ZHAO Lihong (58' REN Liping), LIU Ying (65' ZHANG Ouying),
BAI Jie, SUN Wen. (Coach: MA Liangxing).
Canada: Taryn SWIATEK, Tanya DENNIS, Sharolta Louisa NONEN, Isabelle MORNEAU
(12' Silvana BURTINI), Charmaine HOOPER *(YC76)*, Andrea NEIL *(YC53)*, Diana
MATHESON, Brittany TIMKO, Christine SINCLAIR, Kara Elise LANG *(YC42)* (90' Kristina
KISS), Cristine LATHAM (73' Rhian WILKINSON). (Coach: Even Jostein PELLERUD).
Goal: 7' Charmaine HOOPER 0-1.
Referee: Kari SEITZ (United States)   Attendance: 20.012

SEMI-FINALS

04.10.2003   Providence Park, Portland: Sweden – Canada 2-1 (0-0)
Sweden: Caroline JÖNSSON, Karolina WESTBERG, Jane TÖRNQVIST *(YC64)*, Gärd
Kristin BENGTSSON (75' Sara JOHANSSON), Hanna Gunilla MARKLUND, Frida Christina
ÖSTBERG, Malin Sofi MOSTRÖM, Malin Elisabeth ANDERSSON (70' Kerstin Ingrid
Therese SJÖGRAN), Hanna Carolina LJUNGBERG, Victoria Margareta Sandell SVENSSON,
Anna SJÖSTRÖM (70' Josefine ÖQVIST). (Coach: Marika Susan DOMANSKI LYFORS).
Canada: Taryn SWIATEK, Tanya DENNIS, Sharolta Louisa NONEN, Charmaine HOOPER,
Andrea NEIL, Diana MATHESON, Brittany TIMKO, Christine SINCLAIR, Kara Elise
LANG, Cristine LATHAM (74' Rhian WILKINSON), Silvana BURTINI (55' Kristina KISS).
(Coach: Even Jostein PELLERUD).
Goals: 64' Kara Elise LANG 0-1, 79' Anna SJÖSTRÖM 1-1, 86' Josefine ÖQVIST 2-1.
Referee: Katriina ELOVIRTA (Finland)   Attendance: 27.623

05.10.2003   Providence Park, Portland: United States – Germany 0-3 (0-1)
United States: Briana Collette SCURRY, Catherine WHITEHILL, Kathryn Michele
MARKGRAF Sobrero, Kylie Elizabeth BIVENS (70' Tiffeny Carleen MILBRETT), Joy Lynn
FAWCETT Biefeld, Shannon BOXX, Kristine Marie LILLY Heavey, Julie Maurine FOUDY,
Abby WAMBACH, Mariel Margaret (Mia) HAMM, Cynthia Marie (Cindy) PARLOW Cone
(52' Alyson Kay (Aly) WAGNER). (Coach: April HEINRICHS).
Germany: Silke ROTTENBERG, Kerstin STEGEMANN, Sandra MINNERT, Stefanie
GOTTSCHLICH, Ariane HINGST, Renate LINGOR, Kerstin GAREFREKES, Pia
WUNDERLICH, Maren MEINERT, Bettina WIEGMANN, Birgit PRINZ. (Coach: Tina
THEUNE).
Goals: 15' Kerstin GAREFREKES 0-1, 90+1' Maren MEINERT 0-2, 90+3' Birgit PRINZ 0-3.
Referee: Sonia DENONCOURT (Canada)   Attendance: 27.623

THIRD PLACE MATCH

11.10.2003 Stubhub Center, Carson: United States – Canada 3-1 (1-1)
United States: Briana Collette SCURRY, Christie PEARCE, Catherine WHITEHILL, Kathryn Michele MARKGRAF Sobrero (84' Shannon Ann MACMILLAN), Joy Lynn FAWCETT Biefeld, Shannon BOXX, Kristine Marie LILLY Heavey, Julie Maurine FOUDY (78' Kylie Elizabeth BIVENS), Abby WAMBACH, Mariel Margaret (Mia) HAMM, Cynthia Marie (Cindy) PARLOW Cone (43' Tiffeny Carleen MILBRETT). (Coach: April HEINRICHS).
Canada: Taryn SWIATEK, Kristina KISS, Sharolta Louisa NONEN, Sasha Ajua ANDREWS (84' Isabelle MORNEAU), Charmaine HOOPER (YC76), Andrea NEIL (90' Carmelina MOSCATO), Diana MATHESON, Brittany TIMKO, Christine SINCLAIR, Kara Elise LANG (YC65) (89' Rhian WILKINSON), Cristine LATHAM. (Coach: Even Jostein PELLERUD).
Goals: 22' Kristine Marie LILLY Heavey 1-0, 38' Christine SINCLAIR 1-1, 51' Shannon BOXX 2-1, 80' Tiffeny Carleen MILBRETT 3-1.
Referee: Tammy Nicole OGSTON (Australia)   Attendance: 25.253

FINAL

12.10.2003 Stubhub Center, Carson: Germany – Sweden 2-1 (0-1, 1-1)
Germany: Silke ROTTENBERG, Kerstin STEGEMANN, Sandra MINNERT, Stefanie GOTTSCHLICH, Ariane HINGST, Renate LINGOR, Kerstin GAREFREKES (76' Martina MÜLLER), Pia WUNDERLICH (88' Nia Tsholofelo KÜNZER), Maren MEINERT, Bettina WIEGMANN, Birgit PRINZ. (Coach: Tina THEUNE).
Sweden: Caroline JÖNSSON, Karolina WESTBERG, Jane TÖRNQVIST, Sara LARSSON (76' Gärd Kristin BENGTSSON), Hanna Gunilla MARKLUND, Frida Christina ÖSTBERG, Malin Sofi MOSTRÖM, Malin Elisabeth ANDERSSON (53' Kerstin Ingrid Therese SJÖGRAN), Hanna Carolina LJUNGBERG, Victoria Margareta Sandell SVENSSON, Anna SJÖSTRÖM (53' Linda FAGERSTRÖM). (Coach: Marika Susan DOMANSKI LYFORS).
Goals: 41' Hanna Carolina LJUNGBERG 0-1, 46' Maren MEINERT 1-1, 98' Nia Tsholofelo KÜNZER 2-1.
Referee: Floarea Cristina Ionescu BABADAC (Romania)   Attendance: 26.137

Germany won after extra time.

Germany won the World Cup.

FIFA WOMEN'S WORLD CUP – CHINA PR 2007

GROUP STAGE

GROUP A

10.09.2007 Hongkou Stadium, Shanghai: Germany – Argentina 11-0 (5-0)
Germany: Nadine ANGERER, Kerstin STEGEMANN, Sandra MINNERT, Ariane HINGST,
Renate LINGOR, Kerstin GAREFREKES (84' Anja MITTAG), Melanie BEHRINGER (68'
Petra WIMBERSKY), Linda BRESONIK, Simone LAUDEHR (74' Saskia BARTUSIAK
(YC86)), Birgit PRINZ, Sandra SMISEK. (Coach: Silva NEID).
Argentina: Vanina CORREA, Eva Nadia GONZÁLEZ (YC56), Valeria COTELO, Gabriela
CHAVEZ (YC20), Sabrina BARBITTA, Clarisa HUBER (74' Florencia MANDRILE), Rosana
GÓMEZ (YC16) (66' Mercedes PEREYRA), María Florencia QUIÑONES (YC90+2), Fabiana
VALLEJOS, Analia ALMEYDA (53' Ludmila MANICLER), Belén POTASSA. (Coach: José
Carlos BORRELLO).
Goals: 12' Vanina CORREA 1-0 (og), 17' Kerstin GAREFREKES 2-0,
24' Melanie BEHRINGER 3-0, 29', 45+1' Birgit PRINZ 4-0, 5-0, 51' Renate LINGOR 6-0,
57' Sandra SMISEK 7-0, 59' Birgit PRINZ 8-0, 70', 79' Sandra SMISEK 9-0, 10-0,
90+1' Renate LINGOR 11-0.
Referee: Tammy Nicole OGSTON (Australia)   Attendance: 28.098

11.09.2007   Hongkou Stadium, Shanghai: Japan – England 2-2 (0-0)
Japan: Miho FUKUMOTO, Hiromi ISOZAKI (86' Yuki NAGASATO), Yukari KINGA (46'
Kozue ANDO), Azusa IWASHIMIZU, Tomomi MIYAMOTO (71' Ayumi HARA), Tomoe
KATO Sakai, Homare SAWA, Aya MIYAMA, Rumi UTSUGI, Eriko ARAKAWA, Shinobu
OHNO. (Coach: Hiroshi OHASHI).
England: Rachel Laura BROWN, Alexandra SCOTT (89' Lindsay JOHNSON), Casey
STONEY, Faye Deborah WHITE, Mary Rose PHILLIP, Katie CHAPMAN (YC23), Fara
WILLIAMS, Karen CARNEY, Eniola ALUKO (74' Jill SCOTT), Kelly SMITH (YC90+4),
Rachel YANKEY. (Coach: Hope Patricia POWELL).
Goals: 55' Aya MIYAMA 1-0, 81', 83' Kelly SMITH 1-1, 1-2, 90+5' Aya MIYAMA 2-2.
Referee: Kari SEITZ (United States)   Attendance: 27.146

14.09.2007   Hongkou Stadium, Shanghai: Argentina – Japan 0-1 (0-0)
Argentina: Romina FERRO, Eva Nadia GONZÁLEZ, Gabriela CHAVEZ, Clarisa HUBER
(53' Andrea Susana OJEDA), Catalina PÉREZ, María Florencia QUIÑONES (61' Emilia
MENDIETA), Florencia MANDRILE, Fabiana VALLEJOS, Analia ALMEYDA, Mercedes
PEREYRA, Belén POTASSA (77' Ludmila MANICLER). (Coach: José Carlos BORRELLO).
Japan: Miho FUKUMOTO, Hiromi ISOZAKI (YC57), Kyoko YANO (50' Rumi UTSUGI),
Azusa IWASHIMIZU, Tomomi MIYAMOTO, Tomoe KATO Sakai, Homare SAWA, Aya
MIYAMA, Kozue ANDO (79' Yukari KINGA), Yuki NAGASATO, Shinobu OHNO (57'
Eriko ARAKAWA). (Coach: Hiroshi OHASHI).
Goal: 90+1' Yuki NAGASATO 0-1.
Referee: Dagmar DAMKOVA (Czech Republic)   Attendance: 27.730

14.09.2007   Hongkou Stadium, Shanghai: England – Germany 0-0
England: Rachel Laura BROWN, Alexandra SCOTT, Casey STONEY, Faye Deborah
WHITE, Mary Rose PHILLIP, Anita Amma Ankyewah ASANTE, Katie CHAPMAN *(YC16)*,
Fara WILLIAMS *(YC55)*, Jill SCOTT, Karen CARNEY (57' Rachel YANKEY), Kelly
SMITH. (Coach: Hope Patricia POWELL).
Germany: Nadine ANGERER, Kerstin STEGEMANN, Annike KRAHN *(YC36)*, Ariane
HINGST, Renate LINGOR, Kerstin GAREFREKES, Melanie BEHRINGER (63' Fatmire
ALUSHI *(YC85)*), Linda BRESONIK, Simone LAUDEHR *(YC84)*, Birgit PRINZ, Sandra
SMISEK. (Coach: Silva NEID).
Referee: Jenny PALMQVIST (Sweden)   Attendance: 27.730

17.09.2007   Chengdu Sports Center, Chengdu: England – Argentina 6-1 (2-0)
England: Rachel Laura BROWN, Alexandra SCOTT *(YC4)* (68' Sue SMITH), Casey
STONEY, Faye Deborah WHITE, Mary Rose PHILLIP, Anita Amma Ankyewah ASANTE,
Fara WILLIAMS *(YC61)*, Jill SCOTT, Eniola ALUKO (80' Jodie HANDLEY), Kelly SMITH
(80' Vicky EXLEY), Rachel YANKEY. (Coach: Hope Patricia POWELL).
Argentina: Romina FERRO, Eva Nadia GONZÁLEZ *(YC42)*, Gabriela CHAVEZ, Clarisa
HUBER (52' Valeria COTELO), Catalina PÉREZ *(YC41,YC49)*, María Florencia QUIÑONES
(76' Emilia MENDIETA), Florencia MANDRILE, Fabiana VALLEJOS, Analia ALMEYDA
(62' Natalia GATTI), Mercedes PEREYRA, Belén POTASSA. (Coach: José Carlos
BORRELLO).
Goals: 9' Eva Nadia GONZÁLEZ 1-0 (og), 10' Jill SCOTT 2-0. 50' Fara WILLIAMS 3-0 (p),
60' Eva Nadia GONZÁLEZ 3-1, 64', 77' Kelly SMITH 4-1, 5-1, 90' Vicky EXLEY 6-1 (p).
Referee: Dianne FERREIRA-JAMES (Guyana)   Attendance: 30.730

Sent-off: 49' Catalina PÉREZ.

17.09.2007   Yellow Dragon Sports Center, Hangzhou: Germany – Japan 2-0 (1-0)
Germany: Nadine ANGERER, Kerstin STEGEMANN, Annike KRAHN, Ariane HINGST,
Renate LINGOR, Kerstin GAREFREKES *(YC82)*, Melanie BEHRINGER (57' Fatmire
ALUSHI), Linda BRESONIK, Petra WIMBERSKY, Birgit PRINZ, Sandra SMISEK (78'
Martina MÜLLER *(YC88)*). (Coach: Silva NEID).
Japan: Miho FUKUMOTO, Hiromi ISOZAKI, Yukari KINGA, Azusa IWASHIMIZU, Miyuki
YANAGITA, Ayumi HARA, Tomoe KATO Sakai *(YC16)*, Homare SAWA, Aya MIYAMA
(46' Eriko ARAKAWA, 63' Shinobu OHNO), Rumi UTSUGI, Yuki NAGATO (76'
Tomomi MIYAMOTO). (Coach: Hiroshi OHASHI).
Goals: 21' Birgit PRINZ 1-0, 87' Renate LINGOR 2-0 (p).
Referee: Adriana CORREA (Colombia)   Attendance: 39.817

Team	Pld	W	D	L	GF	GA	GD	Pts
Germany	*3*	*2*	*1*	*0*	*13*	*0*	*13*	*7*
England	*3*	*1*	*2*	*0*	*8*	*3*	*5*	*5*
Japan	3	1	1	1	3	4	-1	4
Argentina	3	0	0	3	1	18	-17	0

51

GROUP B

11.09.2007   Chengdu Sports Center, Chengdu: United States – Korea DPR 2-2 (0-0)
United States: Hope Amelia SOLO, Christie PEARCE *(YC45)*, Catherine WHITEHILL,
Stephanie COX, Kathryn Michele MARKGRAF Sobrero, Shannon BOXX, Kristine Marie
LILLY Heavey, Lori CHALUPNY, Heather O'REILLY (90+2' Natasha KAI), Carli LLOYD,
Abby WAMBACH. (Coach: Greg RYAN).
Korea DPR: JON Myong-Hui, OM Jong-Ran, SONG Jong-Sun, SONU Kyong-Sun, KONG
Hye-Ok, KIM Kyong-Hwa, HO Sun-Hui (22' KIM Yong-Ae, 90' JONG Pok-Sim *(YC90+1)*),
RI Un-Suk, RI Un-Gyong, KIL Son-Hui, RI Kum-Suk. (Coach: KIM Kwang-Min).
Goals: 50' Abby WAMBACH 1-0, 58' KIL Son-Hui 1-1, 62' KIM Yong-Ae 1-2,
69' Heather O'REILLY 2-2.
Referee: Nicole PETIGNAT (Switzerland)   Attendance: 35.100

11.09.2007   Chengdu Sports Center, Chengdu: Nigeria – Sweden 1-1 (0-0)
Nigeria: Predious Uzoaru DEDE, Faith IKIDI, Onome EBI, Ulunma JEROME, Rita
CHIKWELU, Maureen MMADU (59' Efioanwan EKPO), Christie GEORGE, Perpetua
Ijeoma NKWOCHA, Ifeanyi CHIEJINE, Chi-Chi IGBO (35' Stella MBACHU), Cynthia
UWAK. (Coach: Ntiero EFFIOM).
Sweden: Rut Hedvig LINDAHL, Anna PAULSON, Sara Kristina THUNEBRO, Stina
SEGERSTRÖM, Hanna Gunilla MARKLUND, Frida Christina ÖSTBERG, Sara Caroline
SEGER, Kerstin Ingrid Therese SJÖGRAN *(YC12)*, Hanna Carolina LJUNGBERG (69' Sara
JOHANSSON), Victoria Margareta Sandell SVENSSON, Lotta Eva SCHELIN (83' Linda
FORSBERG). (Coach: Thomas DENNERBY).
Goals: 50' Victoria Margareta Sandell SVENSSON 0-1, 82' Cynthia UWAK 1-1.
Referee: NIU Huijun (China PR)   Attendance: 35.600

14.09.2007   Chengdu Sports Center, Chengdu: Sweden- United States 0-2 (0-1)
Sweden: Rut Hedvig LINDAHL, Anna PAULSON, Stina SEGERSTRÖM *(YC34)* (81'
Therese LUNDIN), Hanna Gunilla MARKLUND, Frida Christina ÖSTBERG, Sara Caroline
SEGER *(YC90+3)*, Kerstin Ingrid Therese SJÖGRAN (65' Nilla FISCHER), Hanna Carolina
LJUNGBERG, Linda FORSBERG, Victoria Margareta Sandell SVENSSON, Lotta Eva
SCHELIN. (Coach: Thomas DENNERBY).
United States: Hope Amelia SOLO, Christie PEARCE, Catherine WHITEHILL, Stephanie
COX, Kathryn Michele MARKGRAF Sobrero, Leslie OSBORNE, Kristine Marie LILLY
Heavey, Lori CHALUPNY, Lindsay TARPLEY (67' Heather O'REILLY), Carli LLOYD (46'
Shannon BOXX), Abby WAMBACH. (Coach: Greg RYAN).
Goals: 34', 58' Abby WAMBACH 0-1 (p), 0-2.
Referee: Gyöngyi Krisztina GAÁL (HUN)   Attendance: 35.600

14.09.2007 Chengdu Sports Center, Chengdu: Korea DPR – Nigeria 2-0 (2-0)
Korea DPR: JON Myong-Hui, OM Jong-Ran, SONG Jong-Sun, SONU Kyong-Sun, KONG Hye-Ok, KIM Kyong-Hwa (77' JONG Pok-Sim), RI Un-Suk, RI Un-Gyong, KIL Son-Hui, RI Kum-Suk (YC77), KIM Yong-Ae. (Coach: KIM Kwang-Min).
Nigeria: Predious Uzoaru DEDE, Faith IKIDI, Onome EBI (30' Lilian COLE), Ulunma JEROME (YC52), Rita CHIKWELU (61' Maureen MMADU), Efioanwan EKPO, Christie GEORGE, Perpetua Ijeoma NKWOCHA, Stella MBACHU, Ifeanyi CHIEJINE (YC35) (80' Chi-Chi IGBO), Cynthia UWAK. (Coach: Ntiero EFFIOM).
Goals: 17' KIM Kyong-Hwa 1-0, 21' RI Kum-Suk 2-0.
Referee: Tammy Nicole OGSTON (Australia) Attendance: 35.600

18.09.2007 Tianjin Olympic Center Stadium, Tianjin:
        Korea DPR – Sweden 1-2 (1-1)
Korea DPR: JON Myong-Hui (YC88), OM Jong-Ran, SONG Jong-Sun, SONU Kyong-Sun, KONG Hye-Ok, KIM Kyong-Hwa (56' HONG Myong-Gum), RI Un-Suk, RI Un-Gyong, KIL Son-Hui (85' KIM Ok-Sim), RI Kum-Suk, KIM Yong-Ae (YC32) (60' JONG Pok-Sim). (Coach: KIM Kwang-Min).
Sweden: Rut Hedvig LINDAHL, Anna PAULSON (69' Sara JOHANSSON), Karolina WESTBERG, Nilla FISCHER, Hanna Gunilla MARKLUND, Frida Christina ÖSTBERG (YC31), Sara Caroline SEGER, Kerstin Ingrid Therese SJÖGRAN, Hanna Carolina LJUNGBERG (40' Sara Kristina THUNEBRO, 89' Therese LUNDIN), Victoria Margareta Sandell SVENSSON, Lotta Eva SCHELIN (YC82). (Coach: Thomas DENNERBY).
Goals: 4' Lotta Eva SCHELIN 0-1, 22' RI Un-Suk 1-1, 54' Lotta Eva SCHELIN 1-2.
Referee: Christine BECK (Germany) Attendance: 33.196

18.09.2007 Hongkou Stadium, Shanghai: Nigeria – United States 0-1 (0-1)
Nigeria: Predious Uzoaru DEDE, Faith IKIDI, Ulunma JEROME, Rita CHIKWELU, Lilian COLE (YC14), Efioanwan EKPO, Christie GEORGE, Perpetua Ijeoma NKWOCHA, Stella MBACHU, Chi-Chi IGBO (22' Ifeanyi CHIEJINE), Cynthia UWAK (83' Ogonna CHUKWUDI). (Coach: Ntiero EFFIOM).
United States: Hope Amelia SOLO, Christie PEARCE (77' Tina ELLERTSON), Catherine WHITEHILL, Stephanie COX, Kathryn Michele MARKGRAF Sobrero, Shannon BOXX, Kristine Marie LILLY Heavey (84' Lindsay TARPLEY), Lori CHALUPNY, Heather O'REILLY, Carli LLOYD (64' Leslie OSBORNE), Abby WAMBACH. (Coach: Greg RYAN).
Goal: 1' Lori CHALUPNY 0-1.
Referee: Mayumi OIWA (Japan) Attendance: 6.100

Team	Pld	W	D	L	GF	GA	GD	Pts
United States	3	2	1	0	5	2	3	7
Korea DPR	3	1	1	1	5	4	1	4
Sweden	3	1	1	1	3	4	-1	4
Nigeria	3	0	1	2	1	4	-3	1

GROUP C

12.09.2007   Yellow Dragon Sports Center, Hangzhou: Ghana – Australia 1-4 (0-1)
Ghana: Memunatu SULEMANA, Aminatu IBRAHIM, Mavis DANSO, Olivia AMOAKO,
Yaa AVOE (67' Belinda KANDA), Lydia ANKRAH, Florence OKOE, Adjoa BAYOR,
Memuna DARKU, Anita AMENUKU (67' Hamdya ABASS), Anita AMANKWA. (Coach:
Isaac PAHA).
Australia: Melissa BARBIERI HUDSON, Kate McSHEA *(YC87)*, Dianne ALAGICH, Cheryl
SALISBURY *(YC90)*, Clare POLKINGHORNE (83' Thea SLATYER), Heather GARRIOCK,
Joanne PETERS (62' Alicia FERGUSON), Sally SHIPARD, Caitlin MUNOZ (46' Lisa DE
VANNA), Collette McCALLUM, Sarah WALSH *(YC53)*. (Coach: Tom SERMANNI).
Goals: 15' Sarah WALSH 0-1, 57' Lisa DE VANNA 0-2, 69' Heather GARRIOCK 0-3,
70' Anita AMANKWA 1-3, 81' Lisa DE VANNA 1-4.
Referee: Adriana CORREA (Colombia)   Attendance: 30.752

12.09.2007   Yellow Dragon Sports Center, Hangzhou: Norway – Canada 2-1 (0-1)
Norway: Bente NORDBY, Siri Kristine NORDBY (46' Camilla HUSE), Ane STANGELAND
Horpestad, Trine RØNNING, Gunhild Bentzen FØLSTAD, Ingvild STENSLAND, Leni
LARSEN KAURIN, Solveig GULBRANDSEN, Lene Glesåsen STORLØKKEN (76' Marie
KNUTSEN), Ragnhild Øren GULBRANDSEN, Lindy Melissa Wiik LØVBRÆK (66' Lene
MYKJÅLAND). (Coach: Bjarne BERNTSEN).
Canada: Erin McLEOD, Kristina KISS, Tanya DENNIS, Candace Marie CHAPMAN (73'
Amy Heather WALSH), Martina FRANKO, Randee HERMAS, Diana MATHESON, Sophie
SCHMIDT, Christine SINCLAIR, Melissa TANCREDI (46' Rhian WILKINSON), Kara Elise
LANG (83' Jodi-Ann ROBINSON). (Coach: Even Jostein PELLERUD).
Goals: 33' Candace Marie CHAPMAN 0-1, 52' Ragnhild Øren GULBRANDSEN 1-1,
81' Ane STANGELAND Horpestad 2-1.
Referee: Christine BECK (Germany)   Attendance: 30.752

15.09.2007   Yellow Dragon Sports Center, Hangzhou: Canada – Ghana 4-0 (1-0)
Canada: Erin McLEOD, Kristina KISS, Tanya DENNIS *(YC8)*, Candace Marie CHAPMAN,
Martina FRANKO, Randee HERMAS, Diana MATHESON (84' Andrea NEIL), Katie
THORLAKSON (45' Jodi-Ann ROBINSON), Sophie SCHMIDT, Christine SINCLAIR, Kara
Elise LANG (63' Rhian WILKINSON). (Coach: Even Jostein PELLERUD).
Ghana: Memunatu SULEMANA, Aminatu IBRAHIM, Mavis DANSO, Olivia AMOAKO
(YC78), Yaa AVOE (35' Hamdya ABASS), Florence OKOE, Adjoa BAYOR (71' Safia
ABDULRAHMAN), Memuna DARKU (77' Lydia ANKRAH), Gloria FORIWA *(YC39)*,
Rumanatu TAHIRU, Anita AMANKWA *(YC21)*. (Coach: Isaac PAHA).
Goals: 16' Christine SINCLAIR 1-0, 55' Sophie SCHMIDT 2-0, 62' Christine SINCLAIR 3-0,
77' Martina FRANKO 4-0.
Referee: Nicole PETIGNAT (Switzerland)   Attendance: 33.835

15.09.2007   Yellow Dragon Sports Center, Hangzhou: Australia – Norway 1-1 (0-1)
Australia: Melissa BARBIERI HUDSON, Dianne ALAGICH, Cheryl SALISBURY, Thea
SLATYER, Alicia FERGUSON, Heather GARRIOCK, Lauren Elizabeth COLTHORPE (76'
Caitlin MUNOZ), Danielle SMALL (46' Lisa DE VANNA), Joanne BURGESS, Collette
McCALLUM, Kathryn GILL (61' Sarah WALSH). (Coach: Tom SERMANNI).
Norway: Bente NORDBY, Ane STANGELAND Horpestad, Trine RØNNING, Camilla
HUSE, Gunhild Bentzen FØLSTAD, Ingvild STENSLAND, Leni LARSEN KAURIN (74'
Guro KNUTSEN Mienna), Marie KNUTSEN, Solveig GULBRANDSEN (86' Lene Glesåsen
STORLØKKEN), Ragnhild Øren GULBRANDSEN, Lindy Melissa Wiik LØVBRÆK (46'
Lene MYKJÅLAND). (Coach: Bjarne BERNTSEN).
Goals: 5' Solveig GULBRANDSEN 0-1, 83' Lisa DE VANNA 1-1.
Referee: NIU Huijun (China PR)   Attendance: 33.835

20.09.2007   Yellow Dragon Sports Center, Hangzhou: Norway – Ghana 7-2 (3-0)
Norway: Bente NORDBY, Marit Helene Fiane GRØDUM CHRISTENSEN, Siri Kristine
NORDBY, Ane STANGELAND Horpestad, Camilla HUSE, Ingvild STENSLAND, Leni
LARSEN KAURIN (61' Lise KLAVENESS), Lene MYKJÅLAND (46' Isabell
HERLOVSEN), Solveig GULBRANDSEN (46' Madeleine GISKE), Lene Glesåsen
STORLØKKEN, Ragnhild Øren GULBRANDSEN. (Coach: Bjarne BERNTSEN).
Ghana: Gladys ENTI (64' Memunatu SULEMANA), Aminatu IBRAHIM (YC15), Mavis
DANSO, Olivia AMOAKO, Yaa AVOE, Doreen AWUAH (58' Memuna DARKU), Florence
OKOE, Adjoa BAYOR, Anita AMENUKU (46' Sheila OKAI (YC80)), Rumanatu TAHIRU,
Anita AMANKWA. (Coach: Isaac PAHA).
Goals: 4' Lene Glesåsen STORLØKKEN 1-0, 39' Ragnhild Øren GULBRANDSEN 2-0,
45' Ane STANGELAND Horpestad 3-0 (p), 56' Isabell HERLOVSEN 4-0,
59', 62' Ragnhild Øren GULBRANDSEN 5-0, 6-0, 69' Lise KLAVENESS 7-0,
73' Adjoa BAYOR 7-1, 80' Florence OKOE 7-2 (p).
Referee: Jennifer BENNETT (United States)   Attendance: 43.817

20.09.2007   Chengdu Sports Center, Chengdu: Australia – Canada 2-2 (0-1)
Australia: Melissa BARBIERI HUDSON, Kate McSHEA, Dianne ALAGICH, Cheryl
SALISBURY, Heather GARRIOCK, Joanne PETERS (76' Alicia FERGUSON), Sally
SHIPARD, Lauren Elizabeth COLTHORPE (46' Lisa DE VANNA), Caitlin MUNOZ (62'
Joanne BURGESS), Collette McCALLUM (YC90), Sarah WALSH. (Coach: Tom
SERMANNI).
Canada: Erin McLEOD (79' Taryn SWIATEK), Tanya DENNIS, Rhian WILKINSON,
Candace Marie CHAPMAN, Martina FRANKO, Randee HERMAS (YC89), Diana
MATHESON, Sophie SCHMIDT, Christine SINCLAIR, Melissa TANCREDI (68' Jodi-Ann
ROBINSON), Kara Elise LANG (90+2' Brittany TIMKO). (Coach: Even Jostein
PELLERUD).
Goals: 1' Melissa TANCREDI 0-1, 53' Collette McCALLUM 1-1,
85' Christine SINCLAIR 1-2, 90+2' Cheryl SALISBURY 2-2.
Referee: Gyöngyi Krisztina GAÁL (HUN)   Attendance: 29.300

Team	Pld	W	D	L	GF	GA	GD	Pts
Norway	*3*	*2*	*1*	*0*	*10*	*4*	*6*	*7*
Australia	*3*	*1*	*2*	*0*	*7*	*4*	*3*	*5*
Canada	3	1	1	1	7	4	3	4
Ghana	3	0	0	3	3	15	-12	0

GROUP D

12.09.2007 Wuhan Sports Center Stadium, Wuhan: New Zealand – Brazil 0-5 (0-1)
New Zealand: Jenny Lynn BINDON, Rebecca Katie SMITH, Ria PERCIVAL *(YC25)*, Abby
ERCEG, Alexandra RILEY, Maia Giselle JACKMAN, Katie DUNCAN (66' Priscilla
DUNCAN), Hayley Rose MOORWOOD, Emma HUMPHRIES (72' Zoe Victoria
THOMPSON), Emily McCOLL, Wendi Judith HENDERSON (46' Rebecca TEGG). (Coach:
John HERDMAN).
Brazil: ANDRÉIA Suntaque, ALINE Pellegrino, TÂNIA Maria Pereira Ribeiro,
Renata Aparecida da Costa "KÓKI", Miraildes Maciel Mota "FORMIGA", ESTER Aparecida
dos Santos, SIMONE Gomes Jatobá, DANIELA Alves Lima, ANDRÉIA dos Santos (78'
ROSANA dos Santos Augusto), MARTA Vieira da Silva, CRISTIANE Rozeira de Souza
Silva (84' Delma Gonçalves "PRETINHA"). (Coach: JORGE BARCELLOS).
Goals: 10' DANIELA Alves Lima 0-1, 54' CRISTIANE Rozeira de Souza Silva 0-2,
74' MARTA Vieira da Silva 0-3, 86' Renata Aparecida da Costa "KÓKI" 0-4,
90+3' MARTA Vieira da Silva 0-5.
Referee: Pannipar KAMNUENG (Thailand) Attendance: 50.800

12.09.2007 Wuhan Sports Center Stadium, Wuhan: China PR – Denmark 3-2 (1-0)
China PR: HAN Wenxia, LI Jie (90+3' LIU Yali), WANG Kun, PU Wei, ZHOU Gaoping (68'
ZHANG Ying), XIE Caixia *(YC89)*, BI Yan, PAN Lina, QU Feifei (58' SONG Xiaoli), HAN
Duan, MA Xiaoxu. (Coach: Marika Susan DOMANSKI LYFORS).
Denmark: Heidi ELGAARD-JOHANSEN, Gitte ANDERSEN, Bettina FALK HANSEN, Mia
Birkehøj BROGAARD Olsen, Julie RYDAHL BUKH, Catherine PAASKE SØRENSEN
(YC80), Mariann GAJHEDE Knudsen (75' Stine KJÆR DIMUN), Johanna Maria
Baltensberger RASMUSSEN (75' Merete PEDERSEN), Anne DOT EGGERS NIELSEN,
Katrine Søndergaard PEDERSEN, Maiken With PAPE *(YC86)*. (Coach: Kenneth HEINER-
MØLLER).
Goals: 30' LI Jie 1-0, 50' BI Yan 2-0, 51' Anne DOT EGGERS NIELSEN 2-1,
87' Catherine PAASKE SØRENSEN 2-2, 88' SONG Xiaoli 3-2.
Referee: Dianne FERREIRA-JAMES (Guyana) Attendance: 50.800

15.09.2007   Wuhan Sports Center Stadium, Wuhan:
Denmark – New Zealand 2-0 (0-0)
Denmark: Heidi ELGAARD-JOHANSEN, Gitte ANDERSEN, Bettina FALK HANSEN, Mia
Birkehøj BROGAARD Olsen, Julie RYDAHL BUKH, Catherine PAASKE SØRENSEN (86'
Janne MADSEN), Mariann GAJHEDE Knudsen (46' Maiken With PAPE), Johanna Maria
Baltensberger RASMUSSEN (72' Camilla SAND ANDERSEN), Anne DOT EGGERS
NIELSEN, Katrine Søndergaard PEDERSEN, Merete PEDERSEN. (Coach: Kenneth
HEINER-MØLLER).
New Zealand: Jenny Lynn BINDON *(YC90+2)*, Rebecca Katie SMITH, Ria PERCIVAL (70'
Emma HUMPHRIES), Abby ERCEG *(YC88)*, Marlies OOSTDAM, Alexandra RILEY, Maia
Giselle JACKMAN *(YC60)*, Hayley Rose MOORWOOD (87' Annalie LONGO), Priscilla
DUNCAN, Emily McCOLL, Wendi Judith HENDERSON (64' Rebecca TEGG). (Coach: John
HERDMAN).
Goals: 61' Katrine Søndergaard PEDERSEN 1-0, 66' Catherine PAASKE SØRENSEN 2-0.
Referee: Mayumi OIWA (Japan)   Attendance: 54.000

15.09.2007   Wuhan Sports Center Stadium, Wuhan: Brazil – China PR 4-0 (1-0)
Brazil: ANDRÉIA Suntaque, ELAINE Estrela Moura, ALINE Pellegrino *(YC41)*, TÂNIA
Maria Pereira Ribeiro, Renata Aparecida da Costa "KÓKI" *(YC61)*, Miraildes Maciel Mota
"FORMIGA" (89' SIMONE Gomes Jatobá), ESTER Aparecida dos Santos, DANIELA Alves
Lima *(YC10)* (79' ROSANA dos Santos Augusto), ANDRÉIA dos Santos, MARTA Vieira da
Silva, CRISTIANE Rozeira de Souza Silva (85' KÁTIA Cilene Teixeira da Silva). (Coach:
JORGE BARCELLOS).
China PR: HAN Wenxia, LI Jie, WANG Kun, PU Wei *(YC27)*, LIU Yali (57' ZHOU
Gaoping), SONG Xiaoli, XIE Caixia (67' LIU Sa), BI Yan, PAN Lina (52' ZHANG Tong
(YC53)), HAN Duan, MA Xiaoxu. (Coach: Marika Susan DOMANSKI LYFORS).
Goals: 42' MARTA Vieira da Silva 1-0, 47', 48' CRISTIANE Rozeira de Souza Silva 2-0, 3-0,
70' MARTA Vieira da Silva 4-0.
Referee: Jennifer BENNETT (United States)   Attendance: 54.000

20.09.2007   Yellow Dragon sports Center, Hangzhou: Brazil – Denmark 1-0 (0-0)
Brazil: ANDRÉIA Suntaque, ELAINE Estrela Moura, TÂNIA Maria Pereira Ribeiro,
MÔNICA Angélica de Paula *(YC76)*, Miraildes Maciel Mota "FORMIGA", ESTER Aparecida
dos Santos, SIMONE Gomes Jatobá, DANIELA Alves Lima (88' ROSANA dos Santos
Augusto), ANDRÉIA dos Santos, MARTA Vieira da Silva, CRISTIANE Rozeira de Souza
Silva (61' Delma Gonçalves "PRETINHA"). (Coach: JORGE BARCELLOS).
Denmark: Heidi ELGAARD-JOHANSEN, Gitte ANDERSEN, Christina Øyangen ØRNTOFT,
Mia Birkehøj BROGAARD Olsen, Julie RYDAHL BUKH (65' Johanna Maria Baltensberger
RASMUSSEN), Catherine PAASKE SØRENSEN, Mariann GAJHEDE Knudsen (79' Merete
PEDERSEN), Camilla SAND ANDERSEN (65' Stine KJÆR DIMUN), Anne DOT EGGERS
NIELSEN, Katrine Søndergaard PEDERSEN *(YC42)*, Maiken With PAPE. (Coach: Kenneth
HEINER-MØLLER).
Goal: 90+1' Delma Gonçalves "PRETINHA" 1-0.
Referee: Kari SEITZ (United States)   Attendance: 43.817

20.09.2007   Tianjin Olympic Center Stadium, Tianjin:
China PR – New Zealand 2-0 (0-0)
China PR: ZHANG Yanru, LI Jie, WANG Kun, PU Wei, ZHOU Gaoping (65' LIU Yali
(YC72)), XIE Caixia, BI Yan, PAN Lina (60' ZHANG Tong), HAN Duan, ZHANG Ouying
(88' LIU Sa), MA Xiaoxu. (Coach: Marika Susan DOMANSKI LYFORS).
New Zealand: Jenny Lynn BINDON, Rebecca Katie SMITH, Ria PERCIVAL (73' Merissa
Louise SMITH), Abby ERCEG, Marlies OOSTDAM, Alexandra RILEY, Maia Giselle
JACKMAN, Hayley Rose MOORWOOD *(YC25)*, Priscilla DUNCAN *(YC56)*, Emily
McCOLL (82' Simone CARMICHAEL Ferrara), Wendi Judith HENDERSON (62' Zoe
Victoria THOMPSON). (Coach: John HERDMAN).
Goals: 57' LI Jie 1-0, 79' XIE Caixia 2-0.
Referee: Dagmar DAMKOVA (Czech Republic)   Attendance: 55.832

Team	Pld	W	D	L	GF	GA	GD	Pts
Brazil	*3*	*3*	*0*	*0*	*10*	*0*	*10*	*9*
China PR	*3*	*2*	*0*	*1*	*5*	*6*	*-1*	*6*
Denmark	3	1	0	2	4	4	0	3
New Zealand	3	0	0	3	0	9	-9	0

QUARTER-FINALS

22.09.2007   Wuhan Sports Center Stadium, Wuhan: Germany – Korea DPR 3-0 (1-0)
Germany: Nadine ANGERER, Kerstin STEGEMANN, Annike KRAHN, Ariane HINGST,
Renate LINGOR, Kerstin GAREFREKES, Melanie BEHRINGER, Linda BRESONIK (77'
Sandra MINNERT), Simone LAUDEHR, Birgit PRINZ, Sandra SMISEK (74' Martina
MÜLLER). (Coach: Silva NEID).
Korea DPR: JON Myong-Hui, OM Jong-Ran, SONG Jong-Sun *(YC51)*, SONU Kyong-Sun,
KONG Hye-Ok, HONG Myong-Gum (74' JONG Pok-Sim), RI Un-Suk, RI Un-Gyong, KIL
Son-Hui, RI Kum-Suk, KIM Yong-Ae (50' KIM Kyong-Hwa). (Coach: KIM Kwang-Min).
Goals: 44' Kerstin GAREFREKES 1-0, 67' Renate LINGOR 2-0, 72' Annike KRAHN 3-0.
Referee: Tammy Nicole OGSTON (Australia)   Attendance: 37.200

22.09.2007   Tianjin Olympic Center Stadium, Tianjin:
United States – England 3-0 (0-0)
United States: Hope Amelia SOLO, Christie PEARCE, Catherine WHITEHILL, Stephanie
COX, Kathryn Michele MARKGRAF Sobrero, Shannon BOXX (82' Carli LLOYD), Leslie
OSBORNE, Kristine Marie LILLY Heavey, Lori CHALUPNY, Heather O'REILLY, Abby
WAMBACH (86' Natasha KAI). (Coach: Greg RYAN).
England: Rachel Laura BROWN, Alexandra SCOTT, Casey STONEY, Faye Deborah
WHITE, Mary Rose PHILLIP (80' Lianne SANDERSON), Anita Amma Ankyewah
ASANTE, Katie CHAPMAN, Jill SCOTT, Karen CARNEY, Eniola ALUKO (46' Rachel
YANKEY), Kelly SMITH. (Coach: Hope Patricia POWELL).
Goals: 48' Abby WAMBACH 1-0, 57' Shannon BOXX 2-0, 60' Kristine Marie LILLY
Heavey 3-0.
Referee: Jenny PALMQVIST (Sweden)   Attendance: 29.586

23.09.2007   Wuhan Sports Center Stadium, Wuhan: Norway – China PR 1-0 (1-0)
Norway: Bente NORDBY, Ane STANGELAND Horpestad, Trine RØNNING (YC85),
Camilla HUSE, Gunhild Bentzen FØLSTAD (YC59), Ingvild STENSLAND, Leni LARSEN
KAURIN (64' Lise KLAVENESS), Marie KNUTSEN, Solveig GULBRANDSEN (75' Lene
Glesåsen STORLØKKEN), Ragnhild Øren GULBRANDSEN (YC83), Isabell HERLOVSEN
(90+3' Marit Helene Fiane GRØDUM CHRISTENSEN). (Coach: Bjarne BERNTSEN).
China PR: ZHANG Yanru, LI Jie, WANG Kun (YC69), PU Wei, LIU Yali, XIE Caixia (71'
ZHANG Ouying), BI Yan, PAN Lina, ZHANG Tong (75' LIU Sa), HAN Duan, MA Xiaoxu.
(Coach: Marika Susan DOMANSKI LYFORS).
Goal: 32' Isabell HERLOVSEN 1-0.
Referee: Gyöngyi Krisztina GAÁL (HUN)   Attendance: 52.000

23.09.2007   Tianjin Olympic Center Stadium, Tianjin: Brazil – Australia 3-2 (2-1)
Brazil: ANDRÉIA Suntaque, ELAINE Estrela Moura, ALINE Pellegrino, TÂNIA Maria
Pereira Ribeiro, Renata Aparecida da Costa "KÓKI", Miraildes Maciel Mota "FORMIGA"
(90+2' SIMONE Gomes Jatobá), ESTER Aparecida dos Santos, DANIELA Alves Lima,
ANDRÉIA dos Santos, MARTA Vieira da Silva, CRISTIANE Rozeira de Souza Silva.
(Coach: JORGE BARCELLOS).
Australia: Melissa BARBIERI HUDSON, Dianne ALAGICH, Cheryl SALISBURY (20' Kate
McSHEA), Thea SLATYER, Heather GARRIOCK, Joanne PETERS (YC63) (81' Joanne
BURGESS), Sally SHIPARD (78' Caitlin MUNOZ (YC85)), Lauren Elizabeth COLTHORPE,
Collette McCALLUM, Sarah WALSH, Lisa DE VANNA. (Coach: Tom SERMANNI).
Goals: 4' Miraildes Maciel Mota "FORMIGA" 1-0, 23' MARTA Vieira da Silva 2-0 (p),
36' Lisa DE VANNA 2-1, 68' Lauren Elizabeth COLTHORPE 2-2,
75' CRISTIANE Rozeira de Souza Silva 3-2.
Referee: Christine BECK (Germany)   Attendance: 35.061

59

SEMI-FINALS

26.09.2007   Tianjin Olympic Center Stadium, Tianjin: Germany – Norway 3-0 (1-0)
Germany: Nadine ANGERER, Kerstin STEGEMANN, Annike KRAHN, Ariane HINGST, Renate LINGOR, Kerstin GAREFREKES, Melanie BEHRINGER (40' Fatmire ALUSHI), Linda BRESONIK (81' Sandra MINNERT), Simone LAUDEHR, Birgit PRINZ, Sandra SMISEK (65' Martina MÜLLER). (Coach: Silva NEID).
Norway: Bente NORDBY, Ane STANGELAND Horpestad, Trine RØNNING, Camilla HUSE, Gunhild Bentzen FØLSTAD (48' Siri Kristine NORDBY), Ingvild STENSLAND, Leni LARSEN KAURIN *(YC14)*, Marie KNUTSEN, Solveig GULBRANDSEN (56' Lene Glesåsen STORLØKKEN), Ragnhild Øren GULBRANDSEN, Isabell HERLOVSEN (46' Lise KLAVENESS). (Coach: Bjarne BERNTSEN).
Goals: 42' Trine RØNNING 1-0 (og), 72' Kerstin STEGEMANN 2-0, 75' Martina MÜLLER 3-0.
Referee: Dagmar DAMKOVA (Czech Republic)   Attendance: 53.819

27.09.2007   Yellow Dragon Sports Center, Hangzhou:
          United States – Brazil 0-4 (0-2)
United States: Briana Collette SCURRY, Christie PEARCE, Catherine WHITEHILL, Stephanie COX (46' Carli LLOYD), Kathryn Michele MARKGRAF Sobrero (74' Marian DOUGHERTY), Shannon BOXX *(YC14,YC45+1)*, Leslie OSBORNE, Kristine Marie LILLY Heavey, Lori CHALUPNY *(YC26)*, Heather O'REILLY (60' Tina ELLERTSON), Abby WAMBACH *(YC49)*. (Coach: Greg RYAN).
Brazil: ANDRÉIA Suntaque, ELAINE Estrela Moura, ALINE Pellegrino *(YC28)*, TÂNIA Maria Pereira Ribeiro, Renata Aparecida da Costa "KÓKI" *(YC45)*, Miraildes Maciel Mota "FORMIGA", ESTER Aparecida dos Santos, DANIELA Alves Lima, ANDRÉIA dos Santos, MARTA Vieira da Silva, CRISTIANE Rozeira de Souza Silva. (Coach: JORGE BARCELLOS).
Goals: 20' Leslie OSBORNE 0-1 (og), 27' MARTA Vieira da Silva 0-2, 56' CRISTIANE Rozeira de Souza Silva 0-3, 79' MARTA Vieira da Silva 0-4.
Referee: Nicole PETIGNAT (Switzerland)   Attendance: 47.818

Sent-off: 45+1' Shannon BOXX.

THIRD PLACE MATCH

30.09.2007 Hongkou Stadium, Shanghai: Norway – United States 1-4 (0-1)
Norway: Bente NORDBY, Marit Helene Fiane GRØDUM CHRISTENSEN, Ane
STANGELAND Horpestad, Camilla HUSE, Gunhild Bentzen FØLSTAD (57' Madeleine
GISKE), Ingvild STENSLAND, Marie KNUTSEN, Solveig GULBRANDSEN, Lene Glesåsen
STORLØKKEN (61' Guro KNUTSEN Mienna), Ragnhild Øren GULBRANDSEN, Lindy
Melissa Wiik LØVBRÆK (78' Isabell HERLOVSEN). (Coach: Bjarne BERNTSEN).
United States: Briana Collette SCURRY, Marian DOUGHERTY, Christie PEARCE (46' Tina
ELLERTSON), Catherine WHITEHILL, Stephanie COX, Alyson Kay (Aly) WAGNER (59'
Lindsay TARPLEY), Leslie OSBORNE, Kristine Marie LILLY Heavey (89' Natasha KAI),
Lori CHALUPNY *(YC28)*, Heather O'REILLY, Abby WAMBACH. (Coach: Greg RYAN).
Goals: 30', 46' Abby WAMBACH 0-1, 0-2, 58' Lori CHALUPNY 0-3,
59' Heather O'REILLY 0-4, 63' Ragnhild Øren GULBRANDSEN 1-4.
Referee: Gyöngyi Krisztina GAÁL (HUN)   Attendance: 31.000

FINAL

30.09.2007 Hongkou Stadium, Shanghai: Germany – Brazil 2-0 (0-0)
Germany: Nadine ANGERER, Kerstin STEGEMANN, Annike KRAHN, Ariane HINGST,
Renate LINGOR, Kerstin GAREFREKES *(YC7)*, Melanie BEHRINGER (74' Martina
MÜLLER), Linda BRESONIK *(YC63)*, Simone LAUDEHR, Birgit PRINZ, Sandra SMISEK
(80' Fatmire ALUSHI). (Coach: Silva NEID).
Brazil: ANDRÉIA Suntaque, ELAINE Estrela Moura, ALINE Pellegrino (88' KÁTIA Cilene
Teixeira da Silva), TÂNIA Maria Pereira Ribeiro (81' Delma Gonçalves "PRETINHA"),
Renata Aparecida da Costa "KÓKI", Miraildes Maciel Mota "FORMIGA", ESTER Aparecida
dos Santos (63' ROSANA dos Santos Augusto), DANIELA Alves Lima *(YC59)*, ANDRÉIA
dos Santos, MARTA Vieira da Silva, CRISTIANE Rozeira de Souza Silva. (Coach: JORGE
BARCELLOS).
Goals: 52' Birgit PRINZ 1-0, 86' Simone LAUDEHR 2-0.
Referee: Tammy Nicole OGSTON (Australia)   Attendance: 31.000

Germany retained the World Cup.

FIFA WOMEN'S WORLD CUP – GERMANY 2011

GROUP STAGE

GROUP A

26.06.2011 WIRSOL Rhein-Neckar-Arena, Sinsheim: Nigeria – France 0-1 (0-0)
Nigeria: Predious Uzoaru DEDE, Faith IKIDI (33' Josephine Chiwendu CHUKWUNONYE), Onome EBI, Helen UKAONU, Osinachi Marvis OHALE, Rita CHIKWELU, Glory IROKA, Perpetua Ijeoma NKWOCHA, Stella MBACHU, Ebere ORJI (78' Uchechi Lopez SUNDAY), Ugochi Desire OPARANOZIE (66' Sarah MICHAEL). (Coach: Ngozi UCHE).
France: Bérangère SAPOWICZ, Laura GEORGES, Wendie RENARD (69' Laure Maud Yvette LEPAILLEUR), Sonia BOMPASTOR, Ophelie MEILLEROUX, Camille ABILY, Louisa NECIB, Elise BUSSAGLIA, Sandrine SOUBEYRAND (46' Eugénie LE SOMMER), Marie Laure DELIE, Gaëtane THINEY (57' Elodie THOMIS). (Coaches: Bruno BINI & Corinne DIACRE).
Goal: 56' Marie Laure DELIE 0-1.
Referee: Kari SEITZ (United States) Attendance: 25.475

26.06.2011 Olympiastadion Berlin, Berlin: Germany – Canada 2-1 (2-0)
Germany: Nadine ANGERER, Saskia BARTUSIAK, Babett PETER, Annike KRAHN *(YC90)*, Kerstin GAREFREKES, Melanie BEHRINGER (70' Fatmire ALUSHI), Linda BRESONIK, Simone LAUDEHR *(YC81)*, Kim KULIG, Birgit PRINZ (56' Alexandra POPP), Célia SASIC (65' Inka GRINGS). (Coach: Silva NEID).
Canada: Erin McLEOD, Rhian WILKINSON, Candace Marie CHAPMAN, Emily ZURRER, Marie Eve NAULT (46' Robyn GAYLE), Diana MATHESON, Sophie SCHMIDT, Kaylyn KYLE (46' Kelly PARKER), Christine SINCLAIR, Melissa TANCREDI (80' Brittany TIMKO), Jonelle FILIGNO. (Coach: Carolina MORACE).
Goals: 10' Kerstin GAREFREKES 1-0, 42' Célia SASIC 2-0, 82' Christine SINCLAIR 2-1.
Referee: Jacqui MELKSHAM (Australia) Attendance: 73.680

30.06.2011 Vonovia Ruhrstadion, Bochum: Canada – France 0-4 (0-1)
Canada: Erin McLEOD, Rhian WILKINSON, Candace Marie CHAPMAN, Emily ZURRER, Diana MATHESON *(YC52)*, Brittany TIMKO (77' Chelsea STEWART), Sophie SCHMIDT, Kaylyn KYLE (60' Desiree SCOTT), Christine SINCLAIR, Jonelle FILIGNO, Christina JULIEN (60' Melissa TANCREDI). (Coach: Carolina MORACE).
France: Bérangère SAPOWICZ, Laura GEORGES, Laure Maud Yvette LEPAILLEUR, Sonia BOMPASTOR *(YC37)*, Sabrina Marie-Christine VIGUIER, Camille ABILY (82' Eugénie LE SOMMER), Louisa NECIB, Elise BUSSAGLIA, Sandrine SOUBEYRAND, Marie Laure DELIE (74' Elodie THOMIS), Gaëtane THINEY (79' Laure BOULLEAU). (Coaches: Bruno BINI & Corinne DIACRE).
Goals: 24', 60' Gaëtane THINEY 0-1, 0-2, 67' Camille ABILY 0-3, 83' Elodie THOMIS 0-4.
Referee: Etsuko FUKANO (Japan) Attendance: 16.591

30.06.2011 Commerzbank-Arena, Frankfurt am Main: Germany – Nigeria 1-0 (0-0)
Germany: Nadine ANGERER, Saskia BARTUSIAK, Babett PETER, Annike KRAHN,
Kerstin GAREFREKES, Melanie BEHRINGER (31' Alexandra POPP), Linda BRESONIK,
Simone LAUDEHR, Kim KULIG (YC74), Birgit PRINZ (52' Inka GRINGS), Célia SASIC
(87' Fatmire ALUSHI). (Coach: Silva NEID).
Nigeria: Predious Uzoaru DEDE, Faith IKIDI, Onome EBI, Helen UKAONU, Osinachi
Marvis OHALE (YC50), Rita CHIKWELU, Perpetua Ijeoma NKWOCHA, Stella MBACHU
(85' Francisca ORDEGA), Sarah MICHAEL (70' Uchechi Lopez SUNDAY), Ebere ORJI (62'
Amenze AIGHEWI), Ugochi Desire OPARANOZIE. (Coach: Ngozi UCHE).
Goal: 54' Simone LAUDEHR 1-0.
Referee: CHA Sung-Mi (Korea Republic) Attendance: 48.817

05.07.2011 Stadion im BORUSSIA-PARK, Mönchengladbach:
                    France – Germany 2-4 (0-2)
France: Bérangère SAPOWICZ (RC65), Laura GEORGES (YC41), Laure Maud Yvette
LEPAILLEUR, Wendie RENARD (YC59), Laure BOULLEAU, Louisa NECIB (46' Camille
ABILY), Elodie THOMIS (46' Marie Laure DELIE), Elise BUSSAGLIA (YC40), Sandrine
SOUBEYRAND, Eugénie LE SOMMER (68' Céline DEVILLE goalkeeper), Gaëtane
THINEY. (Coaches: Bruno BINI & Corinne DIACRE).
Germany: Nadine ANGERER, Saskia BARTUSIAK, Babett PETER, Annike KRAHN (78'
Alexandra POPP), Kerstin GAREFREKES, Fatmire ALUSHI (YC82), Simone LAUDEHR
(46' Ariane HINGST), Lena GÖßLING (YC17), Bianca SCHMIDT, Inka GRINGS, Célia
SASIC. (Coach: Silva NEID).
Goals: 25' Kerstin GAREFREKES 0-1, 32' Inka GRINGS 0-2, 56' Marie Laure DELIE 1-2,
68' Inka GRINGS 1-3 (p), 72' Laura GEORGES 2-3, 89' Célia SASIC 2-4.
Referee: Kirsi HEIKKINEN (Finland) Attendance: 45.867

Sent-off: 65' Bérangère SAPOWICZ.

05.07.2011 DDV-Stadion, Dresden: Canada – Nigeria 0-1 (0-0)
Canada: Karina LeBLANC, Rhian WILKINSON, Candace Marie CHAPMAN, Emily
ZURRER, Marie Eve NAULT, Diana MATHESON, Sophie SCHMIDT, Kaylyn KYLE (90'
Desiree SCOTT), Christine SINCLAIR, Melissa TANCREDI (90+6' Jodi-Ann ROBINSON),
Jonelle FILIGNO (56' Christina JULIEN). (Coach: Carolina MORACE).
Nigeria: Predious Uzoaru DEDE, Faith IKIDI, Onome EBI (YC59), Helen UKAONU,
Osinachi Marvis OHALE, Rita CHIKWELU, Glory IROKA, Perpetua Ijeoma NKWOCHA,
Stella MBACHU (82' Francisca ORDEGA), Ebere ORJI (54' Ogonna CHUKWUDI), Ugochi
Desire OPARANOZIE (90+6' Uchechi Lopez SUNDAY). (Coach: Ngozi UCHE).
Goal: 84' Perpetua Ijeoma NKWOCHA 0-1.
Referee: Finau VULIVULI (Fiji) Attendance: 13.638

Team	Pld	W	D	L	GF	GA	GD	Pts
Germany	*3*	*3*	*0*	*0*	*7*	*3*	*4*	*9*
France	*3*	*2*	*0*	*1*	*7*	*4*	*3*	*6*
Nigeria	3	1	0	2	1	2	-1	3
Canada	3	0	0	3	1	7	-6	0

GROUP B

27.06.2011 Vonovia Ruhrstadion, Bochum: Japan – New Zealand 2-1 (1-1)
Japan: Ayumi KAIHORI, Yukari KINGA, Azusa IWASHIMIZU, Aya SAMESHIMA, Saki
KUMAGAI, Homare SAWA, Aya MIYAMA, Mizuho SAKAGUCHI, Kozue ANDO (90+1'
Asuna TANAKA), Yuki NAGASATO (76' Karina MARUYAMA), Shinobu OHNO (55'
Mana IWABUCHI). (Coach: Norio SASAKI).
New Zealand: Jenny Lynn BINDON, Rebecca Katie SMITH *(YC67)*, Ria PERCIVAL (76'
Annalie LONGO), Abby ERCEG, Alexandra RILEY, Anna GREEN, Katie BOWEN *(YC45)*
(46' Hayley Rose MOORWOOD), Katie DUNCAN, Betsy HASSETT, Amber HEARN
(YC77), Sarah GREGORIUS (62' Hannah WILKINSON). (Coach: John HERDMAN).
Goals: 6' Yuki NAGASATO 1-0, 12' Amber HEARN 1-1, 68' Aya MIYAMA 2-1.
Referee: Kirsi HEIKKINEN (Finland) Attendance: 12.538

27.06.2011 VOLKSWAGEN ARENA, Wolfsburg: Mexico – England 1-1 (1-1)
Mexico: Cecilia SANTIAGO Cisneros, Alina Lisi GARCIAMENDEZ Rowold *(YC87)*, Rubí
Marlene SANDOVAL Nungaray, Luz del Rosario SAUCEDO Soto, Natalie Raquel VINTI
Nuno-Vidarte, Nayeli RANGEL Hernandez, Sandra Stephany MAYOR Gutierrez, Teresa
Guadalupe (Lupita) WORBIS Aguilar, Dinora Lizeth GARZA Rodríguez (85' Teresa
NOYOLA Bayardo), Mónica OCAMPO Medina, Maribel Guadalupe DOMÍNGUEZ Castelán
(76' Juana Evelyn LOPEZ Luna). (Coach: Leonardo CUÉLLAR Rivera).
England: Karen BARDSLEY, Alexandra SCOTT, Casey STONEY *(YC88)*, Faye Deborah
WHITE (83' Sophie Elizabeth BRADLEY), Rachel Elizabeth UNITT, Fara WILLIAMS, Jill
SCOTT, Karen CARNEY (72' Ellen WHITE), Eniola ALUKO, Kelly SMITH, Rachel
YANKEY. (Coach: Hope Patricia POWELL).
Goals: 21' Fara WILLIAMS 0-1, 33' Mónica OCAMPO Medina 1-1.
Referee: Silvia Elizabeth REYES (Peru) Attendance: 18.702

01.07.2011 BayArena, Leverkusen: Japan – Mexico 4-0 (3-0)
Japan: Ayumi KAIHORI, Yukari KINGA, Azusa IWASHIMIZU, Aya SAMESHIMA, Saki
KUMAGAI, Homare SAWA (83' Rumi UTSUGI), Aya MIYAMA, Mizuho SAKAGUCHI,
Kozue ANDO (69' Mana IWABUCHI), Yuki NAGASATO, Shinobu OHNO (69' Nahomi
KAWASUMI). (Coach: Norio SASAKI).
Mexico: Cecilia SANTIAGO Cisneros, Alina Lisi GARCIAMENDEZ Rowold, Natalie Ann
GARCIA Mendez, Luz del Rosario SAUCEDO Soto, Natalie Raquel VINTI Nuno-Vidarte,
Nayeli RANGEL Hernandez (46' Liliana MERCADO Fuentes), Sandra Stephany MAYOR
Gutierrez, Dinora Lizeth GARZA Rodríguez, Veronica Raquel PEREZ Murillo (79' Teresa
NOYOLA Bayardo), Mónica OCAMPO Medina, Maribel Guadalupe DOMÍNGUEZ Castelán
(61' Kenti ROBLES Salas). (Coach: Leonardo CUÉLLAR Rivera).
Goals: 13' Homare SAWA 1-0, 15' Shinobu OHNO 2-0, 39',
80' Homare SAWA 3-0, 4-0.
Referee: Christina Westrum PEDERSEN (Norway) Attendance: 22.291

01.07.2011 DDV-Stadion, Dresden: New Zealand – England 1-2 (1-0)
New Zealand: Jenny Lynn BINDON, Rebecca Katie SMITH, Ria PERCIVAL (71' Rosie
WHITE), Abby ERCEG, Alexandra RILEY, Anna GREEN, Katie BOWEN (46' Hayley Rose
MOORWOOD), Katie DUNCAN, Betsy HASSETT, Amber HEARN, Sarah GREGORIUS
(89' Hannah WILKINSON). (Coach: John HERDMAN).
England: Karen BARDSLEY, Alexandra SCOTT, Casey STONEY, Faye Deborah WHITE
(86' Sophie Elizabeth BRADLEY), Rachel Elizabeth UNITT, Fara WILLIAMS, Jill SCOTT,
Eniola ALUKO (46' Karen CARNEY), Kelly SMITH, Rachel YANKEY (66' Jessica Anne
CLARKE), Ellen WHITE. (Coach: Hope Patricia POWELL).
Goals: 18' Sarah GREGORIUS 1-0, 63' Jill SCOTT 1-1, 80' Jessica Anne CLARKE 1-2.
Referee: Therese Raissa NEGUEL (Cameroon) Attendance: 19.110

05.07.2011 WWK Arena, Augsburg: England – Japan 2-0 (1-0)
England: Karen BARDSLEY, Alexandra SCOTT, Casey STONEY, Anita Amma Ankyewah
ASANTE, Rachel Elizabeth UNITT, Sophie Elizabeth BRADLEY, Jill SCOTT, Karen
CARNEY, Kelly SMITH (62' Eniola ALUKO), Jessica Anne CLARKE (46' Rachel
YANKEY), Ellen WHITE (90' Laura BASSETT). (Coach: Hope Patricia POWELL).
Japan: Ayumi KAIHORI, Yukari KINGA, Azusa IWASHIMIZU, Aya SAMESHIMA, Saki
KUMAGAI, Homare SAWA, Aya MIYAMA, Mizuho SAKAGUCHI (74' Mana
IWABUCHI), Kozue ANDO (56' Karina MARUYAMA), Yuki NAGASATO, Shinobu
OHNO (82' Nahomi KAWASUMI). (Coach: Norio SASAKI).
Goals: 15' Ellen WHITE 1-0, 66' Rachel YANKEY 2-0.
Referee: Carol Anne CHENARD (Canada) Attendance: 20.777

05.07.2011 WIRSOL Rhein-Neckar-Arena, Sinsheim:
New Zealand – Mexico 2-2 (0-2)
New Zealand: Jenny Lynn BINDON, Rebecca Katie SMITH, Abby ERCEG, Alexandra
RILEY, Anna GREEN, Katie DUNCAN, Hayley Rose MOORWOOD (60' Kristy YALLOP),
Betsy HASSETT (79' Ria PERCIVAL), Rosie WHITE *(YC33)* (55' Hannah WILKINSON),
Amber HEARN, Sarah GREGORIUS. (Coach: John HERDMAN).
Mexico: Cecilia SANTIAGO Cisneros, Alina Lisi GARCIAMENDEZ Rowold, Kenti
ROBLES Salas (80' Luz del Rosario SAUCEDO Soto), Natalie Ann GARCIA Mendez,
Natalie Raquel VINTI Nuno-Vidarte, Nayeli RANGEL Hernandez (46' Dinora Lizeth GARZA
Rodríguez), Sandra Stephany MAYOR Gutierrez (70' Verónica Charlyn CORRAL Ang),
Teresa Guadalupe (Lupita) WORBIS Aguilar, Veronica Raquel PEREZ Murillo, Mónica
OCAMPO Medina, Maribel Guadalupe DOMÍNGUEZ Castelán *(YC90)*. (Coach: Leonardo
CUÉLLAR Rivera).
Goals: 2' Sandra Stephany MAYOR Gutierrez 0-1, 30' Maribel Guadalupe DOMÍNGUEZ
Castelán 0-2, 90' Rebecca Katie SMITH 1-2, 90+3' Hannah WILKINSON 2-2.
Referee: Jenny PALMQVIST (Sweden) Attendance: 20.451

Team	Pld	W	D	L	GF	GA	GD	Pts
England	*3*	*2*	*1*	*0*	*5*	*2*	*3*	*7*
Japan	*3*	*2*	*0*	*1*	*6*	*3*	*3*	*6*
Mexico	3	0	2	1	3	7	-4	2
New Zealand	3	0	1	2	4	6	-2	1

GROUP C

28.06.2011 BayArena, Leverkusen: Colombia – Sweden 0-1 (0-0)
Colombia: Sandra Milena SEPÚLVEDA Lopera, Andrea Paola PERALTA Delgado (79'
Ingrid Yulieth VIDAL Isaza), Kelis Johana PEDUZINE Vargas, Katherine Nataly ARIAS
Peña, Natalia GAITÁN Laguado, Daniela MONTOYA Quiróz (66' Yulieth Paola
DOMÍNGUEZ Ochoa), Hazleydi Yoreli RINCÓN Torres, Lady Patricia ANDRADE
Rodríguez, Diana Carolina OSPINA García, Maria Catalina USME Pineda (59' Katerin
Fabiola CASTRO Muñoz), Carmen Elisa RODALLEGA. (Coach: Ricardo ROZO Ocampo).
Sweden: Rut Hedvig LINDAHL, Annica SVENSSON, Sara Kristina THUNEBRO, Sara
LARSSON, Barbaro Charlotte ROHLIN, Lisa Karolina Viktoria DAHLKVIST, Sara Caroline
SEGER *(YC29)* (69' Nilla FISCHER), Kerstin Ingrid Therese SJÖGRAN, Jessica
LANDSTRÖM (81' Madeleine EDLUND), Linda FORSBERG (54' Eva Sofia JAKOBSSON),
Lotta Eva SCHELIN. (Coach: Thomas DENNERBY).
Goal: 57' Jessica LANDSTRÖM 0-1.
Referee: Carol Anne CHENARD (Canada) Attendance: 21.106

28.06.2011 DDV-Stadion, Dresden: United States – Korea DPR 2-0 (0-0)
United States: Hope Amelia SOLO, Christie PEARCE, Alexandra Blaire (Ali) KRIEGER, Rachel VAN HOLLEBEKE, Amy LePEILBET, Shannon BOXX, Heather O'REILLY (79' Megan RAPINOE), Carli LLOYD, Abby WAMBACH, Lauren HOLIDAY, Amy RODRIGUEZ (75' Alexandra (Alex) MORGAN). (Coach: Pia Mariane SUNDHAGE).
Korea DPR: HONG Myong-Hui, SONG Jong-Sun, RI Un-Hyang, JO Yun-Mi, RI Ye-Gyong, JON Myong-Hwa (68' KIM Un-Ju), KIM Su-Gyong, JONG Pok-Sim, YUN Hyon-Hi (48' PAEK Sol-Hui), RA Un-Sim, HO Un-Byol (81' KWON Song-Hwa). (Coach: KIM Kwang-Min).
Goals: 54' Lauren HOLIDAY 1-0, 76' Rachel VAN HOLLEBEKE 2-0.
Referee: Bibiana STEINHAUS (Germany) Attendance: 21.859

02.07.2011 WWK Arena, Augsburg: Korea DPR – Sweden 0-1 (0-0)
Korea DPR: HONG Myong-Hui, SONG Jong-Sun, RI Un-Hyang, JO Yun-Mi, RI Ye-Gyong (82' KIM Chung-Sim), JON Myong-Hwa, KIM Su-Gyong (68' KIM Un-Ju), JONG Pok-Sim, YUN Hyon-Hi (79' CHOE Mi-Gyong), RA Un-Sim, HO Un-Byol. (Coach: KIM Kwang-Min).
Sweden: Rut Hedvig LINDAHL, Annica SVENSSON, Sara Kristina THUNEBRO, Sara LARSSON, Barbaro Charlotte ROHLIN, Lisa Karolina Viktoria DAHLKVIST, Sara Caroline SEGER (YC60), Kerstin Ingrid Therese SJÖGRAN (87' Nilla FISCHER), Jessica LANDSTRÖM (76' Josefine ÖQVIST), Linda FORSBERG, Lotta Eva SCHELIN. (Coach: Thomas DENNERBY).
Goal: 64' Lisa Karolina Viktoria DAHLKVIST 0-1.
Referee: Estela ÁLVAREZ (Argentina) Attendance: 23.768

02.07.2011 WIRSOL Rhein-Neckar-Arena, Sinsheim:
        United States – Colombia 3-0 (1-0)
United States: Hope Amelia SOLO, Christie PEARCE, Alexandra Blaire (Ali) KRIEGER, Rachel VAN HOLLEBEKE, Amy LePEILBET (56' Stephanie COX), Lori Ann LINDSEY, Heather O'REILLY (62' Tobin HEATH), Carli LLOYD, Abby WAMBACH, Lauren HOLIDAY, Amy RODRIGUEZ (46' Megan RAPINOE). (Coach: Pia Mariane SUNDHAGE).
Colombia: Sandra Milena SEPÚLVEDA Lopera, Yulieth Paola DOMÍNGUEZ Ochoa, Kelis Johana PEDUZINE Vargas, Fátima MONTAÑO Rentería, Katherine Nataly ARIAS Peña, Natalia GAITÁN Laguado, Liana Milena SALAZAR Vergara (55' Hazleydi Yoreli RINCÓN Torres), Diana Carolina OSPINA García, Maria Catalina USME Pineda (53' Oriánica VELÁSQUEZ Herrera), Carmen Elisa RODALLEGA, Katerin Fabiola CASTRO Muñoz. (Coach: Ricardo ROZO Ocampo).
Goals: 12' Heather O'REILLY 1-0, 50' Megan RAPINOE 2-0, 57' Carli LLOYD 3-0.
Referee: Dagmar DAMKOVA (Czech Republic) Attendance: 25.475

06.07.2011 Vonovia Ruhrstadion, Bochum: Korea DPR – Colombia 0-0
Korea DPR: HONG Myong-Hui, YU Jong-Hee, PAEK Sol-Hui, RI Un-Hyang, JO Yun-Mi, RI
Ye-Gyong, KIM Un-Ju, JON Myong-Hwa, KIM Su-Gyong (48' KIM Chung-Sim), RA Un-
Sim (56' YUN Hyon-Hi, 76' CHOE Mi-Gyong), HO Un-Byol. (Coach: KIM Kwang-Min).
Colombia: Sandra Milena SEPÚLVEDA Lopera, Yulieth Paola DOMÍNGUEZ Ochoa, Kelis
Johana PEDUZINE Vargas, Fátima MONTAÑO Rentería, Katherine Nataly ARIAS Peña,
Natalia GAITÁN Laguado, Daniele MONTOYA Quiróz (89' Liana Milena SALAZAR
Vergara), Diana Carolina OSPINA García, Carmen Elisa RODALLEGA, Oriánica
VELÁSQUEZ Herrera, Katerin Fabiola CASTRO Muñoz (88' Ingrid Yulieth VIDAL Isaza).
(Coach: Ricardo ROZO Ocampo).
Referee: Christina Westrum PEDERSEN (Norway) Attendance: 7.805

06.07.2011 VOLKSWAGEN ARENA, Wolfsburg: Sweden – United States 2-1 (2-0)
Sweden: Rut Hedvig LINDAHL, Annica SVENSSON, Sara Kristina THUNEBRO, Sara
LARSSON, Barbaro Charlotte ROHLIN, Nilla FISCHER (YC60) (88' Linda Brigitta
SEMBRANT), Lisa Karolina Viktoria DAHLKVIST (77' Kristin HAMMARSTRÖM),
Kerstin Ingrid Therese SJÖGRAN (65' Antonia GÖRANSSON), Linda FORSBERG, Josefine
ÖQVIST, Lotta Eva SCHELIN. (Coach: Thomas DENNERBY).
United States: Hope Amelia SOLO, Christie PEARCE, Alexandra Blaire (Ali) KRIEGER,
Rachel VAN HOLLEBEKE, Amy LePEILBET (YC14) (59' Stephanie COX), Shannon
BOXX, Carli LLOYD, Abby WAMBACH, Lauren HOLIDAY, Megan RAPINOE (73' Kelly
O'HARA), Amy RODRIGUEZ (46' Alexandra (Alex) MORGAN). (Coach: Pia Mariane
SUNDHAGE).
Goals: 16' Lisa Karolina Viktoria DAHLKVIST 1-0 (p), 35' Nilla FISCHER 2-0,
67' Abby WAMBACH 2-1.
Referee: Etsuko FUKANO (Japan) Attendance: 23.468

Team	Pld	W	D	L	GF	GA	GD	Pts
Sweden	3	3	0	0	4	1	3	9
United States	3	2	0	1	6	2	4	6
Korea DPR	3	0	1	2	0	3	-3	1
Colombia	3	0	1	2	0	4	-4	1

GROUP D

29.06.2011 WWK Arena, Augsburg: Norway – Equatorial Guinea 1-0 (0-0)
Norway: Ingrid HJELMSETH, Hedda Strand GARDSJORD, Nora Holstad BERGE, Trine RØNNING, Marita Skammelsrud LUND, Maren MJELDE *(YC63)*, Ingvild STENSLAND, Madeleine GISKE (46' Lene MYKJÅLAND, 70' Leni LARSEN KAURIN), Isabell HERLOVSEN (62' Cecilie PEDERSEN), Elise THORSNES *(YC90+2)*, Emilie HAAVI. (Coach: Eli LANDSEM).
Equatorial Guinea: MIRIAM Silva da Paixão, Carolina Conceição Martins de Pereira "CAROL CARIOCA", BRUNA Amarante da Silva, Dúlcia Maria Davi "DULCE", Ana Cristina da Silva "CRIS", DORINE Nina Chuigoue, Jumária Barbosa de Santana "JU" (52' Gloria CHINASA Okoro), Olive CHRISTELLE Ngo Nyepel (46' LAETITIA Chapeh Yimga), GENOVEVA AÑONMA, VANIA Cristina Martins, DIALA Blessing (65' ADRIANA Aparecida Costa). (Coach: MARCELO FRIGERIO).
Goal: 84 Emilie HAAVI 1-0.
Referee: Quetzalli ALVARADO Godínez (Mexico) Attendance: 12.928

29.06.2011 Stadion im BORUSSIA-PARK, Mönchengladbach:
Brazil – Australia 1-0 (0-0)
Brazil: ANDRÉIA Suntaque, ALINE Pellegrino, ÉRIKA Cristiano dos Santos, FABIANA da Silva Simões, DAIANE Menezes Ridrigues, ROSANA dos Santos Augusto, Miraildes Maciel Mota "FORMIGA" (84' FRANCIELLE Manoel Alberto), ESTER Aparecida dos Santos, MAURINE Dornelles Gonçalves, MARTA Vieira da Silva, CRISTIANE Rozeira de Souza Silva. (Coaches: KLEITON Barbosa de Oliveira LIMA & JORGE BARCELLOS).
Australia: Melissa BARBIERI HUDSON, Emily VAN EGMOND (61' Sally SHIPARD), Kim CARROLL, Servet UZUNLAR, Heather GARRIOCK, Elise KELLOND, Tameka BUTT (86' Clare POLKINGHORNE), Collette McCALLUM, Lisa DE VANNA, Kyah SIMON (79' Samantha KERR), Caitlin FOORD. (Coach: Tom SERMANNI).
Goal: 54' ROSANA dos Santos Augusto 1-0.
Referee: Jenny PALMQVIST (Sweden) Attendance: 27.258

03.07.2011 Vonovia Ruhrstadion, Bochum: Australia – Equatorial Guinea 3-2 (1-1)
Australia: Lydia WILLIAMS, Emily VAN EGMOND, Kim CARROLL, Servet UZUNLAR, Heather GARRIOCK, Sally SHIPARD (46' Lisa DE VANNA *(YC72)*), Lauren Elizabeth COLTHORPE, Elise KELLOND, Collette McCALLUM (78' Clare POLKINGHORNE), Leena KHAMIS, Samantha KERR (69' Teigen ALLEN). (Coach: Tom SERMANNI).
Equatorial Guinea: MIRIAM Silva da Paixão, Carolina Conceição Martins de Pereira "CAROL CARIOCA", BRUNA Amarante da Silva (82' LAETITIA Chapeh Yimga), Dúlcia Maria Davi "DULCE", Ana Cristina da Silva "CRIS" *(YC47)*, DORINE Nina Chuigoue, Jumária Barbosa de Santana "JU" (65' SINFOROSA Eyang Nguema Nchama *(YC79)*), Gloria CHINASA Okoro (57' ADRIANA Aparecida Costa), GENOVEVA AÑONMA *(YC41)*, VANIA Cristina Martins, DIALA Blessing. (Coach: MARCELO FRIGERIO).
Goals: 8' Leena KHAMIS 1-0, 21' GENOVEVA AÑONMA 1-1,
48' Emily VAN EGMOND 2-1, 51' Lisa DE VANNA 3-1, 83' GENOVEVA AÑONMA 3-2.
Referee: Gyöngyi Krisztina GAÁL (HUN) Attendance: 15.640

69

03.07.2011 VOLKSWAGEN ARENA, Wolfsburg: Brazil – Norway 3-0 (1-0)
Brazil: ANDRÉIA Suntaque, ALINE Pellegrino, ÉRIKA Cristiano dos Santos, FABIANA da
Silva Simões (76' FRANCIELLE Manoel Alberto), DAIANE Menezes Ridrigues *(YC19)* (84'
Renata Aparecida da Costa "KÓKI"), ROSANA dos Santos Augusto, Miraildes Maciel Mota
"FORMIGA", ESTER Aparecida dos Santos (89' GRAZIELLE Pinheiro Nascimento),
MAURINE Dornelles Gonçalves, MARTA Vieira da Silva, CRISTIANE Rozeira de Souza
Silva. (Coaches: KLEITON Barbosa de Oliveira LIMA & JORGE BARCELLOS).
Norway: Ingrid HJELMSETH, Nora Holstad BERGE, Trine RØNNING, Marita Skammelsrud
LUND, Maren MJELDE, Ingvild STENSLAND (67' Gry Tofte IMS), Leni LARSEN
KAURIN (46' Elise THORSNES), Guro KNUTSEN Mienna, Madeleine GISKE, Isabell
HERLOVSEN, Emilie HAAVI (52' Cecilie PEDERSEN). (Coach: Eli LANDSEM).
Goals: 22' MARTA Vieira da Silva 1-0, 46' ROSANA dos Santos Augusto 2-0,
48' MARTA Vieira da Silva 3-0.
Referee: Kari SEITZ (United States) Attendance: 26.067

06.07.2011 BayArena, Leverkusen: Australia – Norway 2-1 (0-0)
Australia: Melissa BARBIERI HUDSON, Clare POLKINGHORNE, Kim CARROLL
(YC45+3), Servet UZUNLAR, Heather GARRIOCK *(YC68)*, Elise KELLOND, Collette
McCALLUM, Lisa DE VANNA, Samantha KERR (81' Laura ALLEWAY), Kyah SIMON,
Caitlin FOORD (90' Ellyse PERRY). (Coach: Tom SERMANNI).
Norway: Ingrid HJELMSETH (46' Erika Espeseth SKARBØ), Hedda Strand GARDSJORD
(YC90+2), Trine RØNNING, Maren MJELDE, Ingvild STENSLAND, Lene MYKJÅLAND,
Guro KNUTSEN Mienna, Gry Tofte IMS (82' Isabell HERLOVSEN), Elise THORSNES,
Emilie HAAVI (46' Kristine MINDE), Cecilie PEDERSEN. (Coach: Eli LANDSEM).
Goals: 56' Elise THORSNES 0-1, 57', 87' Kyah SIMON 1-1, 2-1.
Referee: Estela ÁLVAREZ (Argentina) Attendance: 18.474

06.07.2011 Commerzbank-Arena, Frankfurt am Main:
         Equatorial Guinea – Brazil 0-3 (0-0)
Equatorial Guinea: MIRIAM Silva da Paixão, Carolina Conceição Martins de Pereira "CAROL
CARIOCA", BRUNA Amarante da Silva *(YC90+3)*, Dúlcia Maria Davi "DULCE" *(YC9)*,
LAETITIA Chapeh Yimga, Ana Cristina da Silva "CRIS" (71' SINFOROSA Eyang Nguema
Nchama), DORINE Nina Chuigoue, Jumária Barbosa de Santana "JU", GENOVEVA
AÑONMA, VANIA Cristina Martins, DIALA Blessing *(YC60)* (86' ADRIANA Aparecida
Costa). (Coach: MARCELO FRIGERIO).
Brazil: ANDRÉIA Suntaque, ALINE Pellegrino, Renata Aparecida da Costa "KÓKI" *(YC77)*,
ÉRIKA Cristiano dos Santos, FABIANA da Silva Simões (82' THAIS Duarte GUEDES),
ROSANA dos Santos Augusto (70' FRANCIELLE Manoel Alberto *(YC74)*), Miraildes Maciel
Mota "FORMIGA" (90' BEATRIZ Zaneratto João), ESTER Aparecida dos Santos,
MAURINE Dornelles Gonçalves, MARTA Vieira da Silva, CRISTIANE Rozeira de Souza
Silva. (Coaches: KLEITON Barbosa de Oliveira LIMA & JORGE BARCELLOS).
Goals: 49' ÉRIKA Cristiano dos Santos 0-1, 54',
90+3' CRISTIANE Rozeira de Souza Silva 0-2, 0-3 (p).
Referee: Bibiana STEINHAUS (Germany) Attendance: 35.859

Team	Pld	W	D	L	GF	GA	GD	Pts
Brazil	*3*	*3*	*0*	*0*	*7*	*0*	*7*	*9*
Australia	*3*	*2*	*0*	*1*	*5*	*4*	*1*	*6*
Norway	3	1	0	2	2	5	-3	3
Equatorial Guinea	3	0	0	3	2	7	-5	0

QUARTER-FINALS

09.07.2011 BayArena, Leverkusen: England – France 1-1 (0-0, 1-1)
England: Karen BARDSLEY *(YC87)*, Alexandra SCOTT (81' Stephanie HOUGHTON), Casey STONEY, Faye Deborah WHITE, Rachel Elizabeth UNITT (82' Claire RAFFERTY), Fara WILLIAMS *(YC5)*, Jill SCOTT *(YC90+3)*, Karen CARNEY, Kelly SMITH, Rachel YANKEY (84' Anita Amma Ankyewah ASANTE), Ellen WHITE *(YC77)*. (Coach: Hope Patricia POWELL).
France: Céline DEVILLE, Laura GEORGES, Laure Maud Yvette LEPAILLEUR, Sonia BOMPASTOR, Sabrina Marie-Christine VIGUIER, Camille ABILY, Louisa NECIB (79' Sandrine BRÉTIGNY, 106' Eugénie LE SOMMER), Elise BUSSAGLIA, Sandrine SOUBEYRAND (67' Elodie THOMIS), Marie Laure DELIE, Gaëtane THINEY. (Coaches: Bruno BINI & Corinne DIACRE).
Goals: 59' Jill SCOTT 1-0, 88' Elise BUSSAGLIA 1-1.
Referee: Jenny PALMQVIST (Sweden)   Attendance: 26.395

Penalties: Camille ABILY missed, Kelly SMITH 0-1, Elise BUSSAGLIA 1-1, Karen CARNEY 1-2, Gaëtane THINEY 2-2, Casey STONEY 2-3, Sonia BOMPASTOR 3-3, Claire RAFFERTY missed, Eugénie LE SOMMER 3-4, Faye Deborah WHITE missed.

After extra time, France won 4-3 on penalties.

09.07.2011 VOLKSWAGEN ARENA, Wolfsburg: Germany – Japan 0-1 (0-0, 0-0)
Germany: Nadine ANGERER, Saskia BARTUSIAK, Babett PETER *(YC105)*, Annike KRAHN, Kerstin GAREFREKES, Melanie BEHRINGER, Linda BRESONIK (64' Lena GÖßLING), Simone LAUDEHR, Kim KULIG (8' Bianca SCHMIDT), Inka GRINGS (102' Alexandra POPP), Célia SASIC. (Coach: Silva NEID).
Japan: Ayumi KAIHORI, Yukari KINGA, Azusa IWASHIMIZU *(YC55)*, Aya SAMESHIMA, Saki KUMAGAI *(YC114)*, Homare SAWA *(YC87)*, Aya MIYAMA, Mizuho SAKAGUCHI *(YC72)*, Kozue ANDO, Yuki NAGASATO (46' Karina MARUYAMA), Shinobu OHNO (65' Mana IWABUCHI, 116' Rumi UTSUGI). (Coach: Norio SASAKI).
Goal: 108' Karina MARUYAMA 0-1.
Referee: Quetzalli ALVARADO Godínez (Mexico)   Attendance: 26.067

Japan won after extra time.

10.07.2011 WWK Arena, Augsburg: Sweden – Australia 3-1 (2-1)
Sweden: Rut Hedvig LINDAHL, Annica SVENSSON (90+2' Lina Therese NILSSON), Sara
Kristina THUNEBRO, Sara LARSSON, Barbaro Charlotte ROHLIN, Lisa Karolina Viktoria
DAHLKVIST, Sara Caroline SEGER, Kerstin Ingrid Therese SJÖGRAN *(YC67)*, Linda
FORSBERG (67' Nilla FISCHER *(YC81)*), Josefine ÖQVIST (83' Madeleine EDLUND),
Lotta Eva SCHELIN. (Coach: Thomas DENNERBY).
Australia: Melissa BARBIERI HUDSON, Emily VAN EGMOND (58' Clare
POLKINGHORNE), Kim CARROLL, Ellyse PERRY (59' Tameka BUTT), Servet
UZUNLAR, Heather GARRIOCK *(YC80)*, Elise KELLOND, Collette McCALLUM (79' Sally
SHIPARD), Lisa DE VANNA, Kyah SIMON *(YC23)*, Caitlin FOORD. (Coach: Tom
SERMANNI).
Goals: 11' Kerstin Ingrid Therese SJÖGRAN 1-0, 16' Lisa Viktoria DAHLKVIST 2-0,
40' Ellyse PERRY 2-1, 52' Lotta Eva SCHELIN 3-1.
Referee: Silvia Elizabeth REYES (Peru) Attendance: 24.605

10.07.2011 DDV-Stadion, Dresden: Brazil – United States 2-2 (0-1, 1-1)
Brazil: ANDRÉIA Suntaque, ALINE Pellegrino *(YC44)*, ÉRIKA Cristiano dos Santos
(YC117), FABIANA da Silva Simões, DAIANE Menezes Ridrigues, ROSANA dos Santos
Augusto (85' FRANCIELLE Manoel Alberto), Miraildes Maciel Mota "FORMIGA" (113'
Renata Aparecida da Costa "KÓKI"), ESTER Aparecida dos Santos, MAURINE Dornelles
Gonçalves *(YC112)*, MARTA Vieira da Silva *(YC45)*, CRISTIANE Rozeira de Souza Silva.
(Coaches: KLEITON Barbosa de Oliveira LIMA & JORGE BARCELLOS).
United States: Hope Amelia SOLO *(YC67)*, Christie PEARCE, Alexandra Blaire (Ali)
KRIEGER, Rachel VAN HOLLEBEKE *(RC66)*, Amy LePEILBET, Shannon BOXX *(YC113)*,
Heather O'REILLY (108' Tobin HEATH), Carli LLOYD *(YC29)*, Abby WAMBACH, Lauren
HOLIDAY (55' Megan RAPINOE *(YC90)*), Amy RODRIGUEZ (72' Alexandra (Alex)
MORGAN). (Coach: Pia Mariane SUNDHAGE).
Goals: 2' DAIANE Menezes Ridrigues 0-1 (og), 68', 92' MARTA Vieira da Silva 1-1 (p), 2-1,
120+2' Abby WAMBACH 2-2.
Referee: Jacqui MELKSHAM (Australia) Attendance: 25.598

Sent-off: 66' Rachel VAN HOLLEBEKE.

Penalties: Shannon BOXX 1-0, CRISTIANE Rozeira de Souza Silva 1-1, Carli LLOYD
2-1, MARTA Vieira da Silva 2-2, Abby WAMBACH 3-2, DAIANE Menezes
Ridrigues missed, Megan RAPINOE 4-2, FRANCIELLE Manoel Alberto
4-3, Alexandra Blaire (Ali) KRIEGER 5-3.

After extra time, the United States won 5-3 on penalties.

SEMI-FINALS

13.07.2011   Stadion im BORUSSIA-PARK, Mönchengladbach:
        France – United States 1-3 (0-1)
France: Bérangère SAPOWICZ, Laura GEORGES, Laure Maud Yvette LEPAILLEUR, Sonia
BOMPASTOR, Ophelie MEILLEROUX, Camille ABILY, Louisa NECIB, Elise
BUSSAGLIA, Sandrine SOUBEYRAND (78' Elodie THOMIS *(YC90)*), Marie Laure DELIE
(46' Eugénie LE SOMMER), Gaëtane THINEY. (Coaches: Bruno BINI & Corinne DIACRE).
United States: Hope Amelia SOLO, Christie PEARCE, Alexandra Blaire (Ali) KRIEGER,
Becky SAUERBRUNN, Amy LePEILBET, Shannon BOXX, Heather O'REILLY (87' Tobin
HEATH), Carli LLOYD (65' Megan RAPINOE), Abby WAMBACH, Lauren HOLIDAY,
Amy RODRIGUEZ (56' Alexandra (Alex) MORGAN). (Coach: Pia Mariane SUNDHAGE).
Goals: 9' Lauren HOLIDAY 0-1, 55' Sonia BOMPASTOR 1-1, 79' Abby WAMBACH 1-2,
82' Alexandra (Alex) MORGAN 1-3.
Referee: Kirsi HEIKKINEN (Finland)   Attendance: 25.676

13.07.2011   Commerzbank-Arena, Frankfurt am Main: Japan – Sweden 3-1 (1-1)
Japan: Ayumi KAIHORI, Yukari KINGA, Azusa IWASHIMIZU, Aya SAMESHIMA, Saki
KUMAGAI, Homare SAWA, Aya MIYAMA (89' Megumi KAMIONOBE), Mizuho
SAKAGUCHI, Kozue ANDO, Shinobu OHNO (86' Megumi TAKASE), Nahomi
KAWASUMI (74' Yuki NAGASATO). (Coach: Norio SASAKI).
Sweden: Rut Hedvig LINDAHL, Annica SVENSSON *(YC70)*, Sara Kristina THUNEBRO,
Sara LARSSON, Barbaro Charlotte ROHLIN, Lisa Karolina Viktoria DAHLKVIST, Marie
HAMMARSTRÖM (69' Jessica LANDSTRÖM), Kerstin Ingrid Therese SJÖGRAN, Linda
FORSBERG (65' Eva Sofia JAKOBSSON), Josefine ÖQVIST (75' Antonia GÖRANSSON),
Lotta Eva SCHELIN. (Coach: Thomas DENNERBY).
Goals: 10' Josefine ÖQVIST 0-1, 19' Nahomi KAWASUMI 1-1, 60' Homare SAWA 2-1,
64' Nahomi KAWASUMI 3-1.
Referee: Carol Anne CHENARD (Canada)   Attendance: 45.434

73

THIRD PLACE MATCH

16.07.2011 WIRSOL Rhein-Neckar-Arena, Sinsheim: Sweden – France 2-1 (1-0)
Sweden: Rut Hedvig LINDAHL, Annica SVENSSON, Sara Kristina THUNEBRO, Sara
LARSSON, Barbaro Charlotte ROHLIN, Nilla FISCHER (73' Linda Brigitta SEMBRANT),
Lisa Karolina Viktoria DAHLKVIST, Kerstin Ingrid Therese SJÖGRAN, Linda FORSBERG
(62' Marie HAMMARSTRÖM), Josefine ÖQVIST *(RC68)*, Lotta Eva SCHELIN. (Coach:
Thomas DENNERBY).
France: Bérangère SAPOWICZ (32' Céline DEVILLE), Laura GEORGES, Wendie RENARD,
Sonia BOMPASTOR, Corine PETIT-FRANCO (84' Caroline PIZZALA), Camille ABILY,
Louisa NECIB (32' Elodie THOMIS), Elise BUSSAGLIA, Sandrine SOUBEYRAND,
Eugénie LE SOMMER, Gaëtane THINEY. (Coaches: Bruno BINI & Corinne DIACRE).
Goals: 29' Lotta Eva SCHELIN 1-0, 56' Elodie THOMIS 1-1,
82' Marie HAMMARSTRÖM 2-1.
Referee: Kari SEITZ (United States) Attendance: 25.475

Sent-off: 68' Josefine ÖQVIST.

FINAL

17.07.2011 Commerzbank-Arena, Frankfurt am Main:
Japan – United States 2-2 (0-0, 1-1)
Japan: Ayumi KAIHORI, Yukari KINGA, Azusa IWASHIMIZU *(RC120+1)*, Aya
SAMESHIMA, Saki KUMAGAI, Homare SAWA, Aya MIYAMA *(YC97)*, Mizuho
SAKAGUCHI, Kozue ANDO (66' Yuki NAGASATO), Shinobu OHNO (66' Karina
MARUYAMA, 119' Mana IWABUCHI), Nahomi KAWASUMI. (Coach: Norio SASAKI).
United States: Hope Amelia SOLO, Christie PEARCE, Alexandra Blaire (Ali) KRIEGER,
Rachel VAN HOLLEBEKE, Amy LePEILBET, Shannon BOXX, Heather O'REILLY, Carli
LLOYD, Abby WAMBACH, Lauren HOLIDAY (46' Alexandra (Alex) MORGAN), Megan
RAPINOE (114' Tobin HEATH). (Coach: Pia Mariane SUNDHAGE).
Goals: 68' Alexandra (Alex) MORGAN 0-1, 81' Aya MIYAMA 1-1,
104' Abby WAMBACH 1-2, 117' Homare SAWA 2-2.
Referee: Bibiana STEINHAUS (Germany) Attendance: 48.817

Sent-off: 120+1' Azusa IWASHIMIZU.

Penalties: Shannon BOXX missed, Aya MIYAMA 0-1, Carli LLOYD missed, Yuki
NAGASATO missed, Tobin HEATH missed, Mizuho SAKAGUCHI 0-2,
Abby WAMBACH 1-2, Saki KUMAGAI 1-3.

After extra time, Japan won 3-1 on penalties.

Japan won the World Cup.

74

FIFA WOMEN'S WORLD CUP – CANADA 2015

GROUP STAGE

GROUP A

06.06.2015 Commonwealth Stadium, Edmonton: Canada – China PR 1-0 (0-0)
Canada: Erin McLEOD, Lauren SESSELMANN, Josee BELANGER, Allysha CHAPMAN, Kadiesha BUCHANAN, Sophie SCHMIDT, Ashley LAWRENCE, Desiree SCOTT *(YC22)* (71' Jessie FLEMING), Christine SINCLAIR, Melissa TANCREDI (77' Adriana LEON), Jonelle FILIGNO (61' Kaylyn KYLE). (Coach: John HERDMAN).
China PR: WANG Fei, LI Dongna, WU Haiyan, LIU Shanshan, WANG Shanshan, REN Guixin, TAN Ruyin, WANG Lisi (42' HAN Peng), GU Yasha (87' MA Jun), LI Ying (62' ZHANG Rui), ZHAO Rong. (Coach: HAO Wei).
Goal: 90+2' Christine SINCLAIR 1-0.
Referee: Kateryna MONZUL (Ukraine) Attendance: 53.058

06.06.2015 Commonwealth Stadium, Edmonton:
New Zealand – Netherlands 0-1 (0-1)
New Zealand: Erin NAYLER, Ria PERCIVAL, Abby ERCEG, Alexandra RILEY, Katie BOWEN (72' Betsy HASSETT), Rebekah STOTT, Katie DUNCAN, Annalie LONGO, Amber HEARN, Hannah WILKINSON, Sarah GREGORIUS (67' Jasmine PEREIRA). (Coach: Tony READINGS).
Netherlands: Loes GEURTS, Mandy VAN DEN BERG, Petra HOGEWONING, Stephanie VAN DER GRAGT, Anouk DEKKER (84' Tessel MIDDAG), Sherida SPITSE, Danielle VAN DE DONK *(YC32)*, Desiree VAN LUNTEREN, Lieke MARTENS *(YC64)* (90+2' Kirsten VAN DE VEN), Manon MELIS, Vivianne MIEDEMA (81' Shanice VAN DE SANDEN). (Coach: Roger REIJNERS).
Goal: 33' Lieke MARTENS 0-1.
Referee: Quetzalli ALVARADO Godínez (Mexico) Attendance: 53.058

11.06.2015 Commonwealth Stadium, Edmonton: China PR – Netherlands 1-0 (0-0)
China PR: WANG Fei, LI Dongna, WU Haiyan, LIU Shanshan, WANG Shanshan (57' WANG Shuang), TANG Jiali (86' LOU Jiahui), HAN Peng, REN Guixin (71' MA Jun), TAN Ruyin, WANG Lisi, ZHAO Rong. (Coach: HAO Wei).
Netherlands: Sari VAN VEENENDAAL, Mandy VAN DEN BERG, Petra HOGEWONING (59' Merel VAN DONGEN), Stephanie VAN DER GRAGT, Sherida SPITSE, Danielle VAN DE DONK, Desiree VAN LUNTEREN, Lieke MARTENS, Tessel MIDDAG (70' Anouk DEKKER), Manon MELIS, Vivianne MIEDEMA. (Coach: Roger REIJNERS).
Goal: 90+1' WANG Lisi 1-0.
Referee: Yeimi Lucero MARTÍNEZ Valverde (Colombia) Attendance: 35.544

11.06.2015   Commonwealth Stadium, Edmonton: Canada – New Zealand 0-0
Canada: Erin McLEOD, Lauren SESSELMANN (68' Carmelina MOSCATO), Josee
BELANGER, Allysha CHAPMAN *(YC31)*, Kadiesha BUCHANAN, Sophie SCHMIDT,
Ashley LAWRENCE, Desiree SCOTT (73' Adriana LEON), Christine SINCLAIR, Melissa
TANCREDI, Jonelle FILIGNO (63' Kaylyn KYLE). (Coach: John HERDMAN).
New Zealand: Erin NAYLER, Ria PERCIVAL *(YC52)*, Abby ERCEG, Alexandra RILEY,
Rebekah STOTT, Katie DUNCAN, Annalie LONGO, Betsy HASSETT (77' Katie BOWEN),
Amber HEARN, Hannah WILKINSON (89' Jasmine PEREIRA), Sarah GREGORIUS *(YC71)*
(80' Rosie WHITE). (Coach: Tony READINGS).
Referee: Bibiana STEINHAUS (Germany)   Attendance: 35.544

Amber HEARN missed a penalty kick (32').

15.06.2015   Stade Olympique, Montréal: Netherlands – Canada 1-1 (0-1)
Netherlands: Loes GEURTS, Mandy VAN DEN BERG, Stephanie VAN DER GRAGT
(YC73), Merel VAN DONGEN, Anouk DEKKER, Sherida SPITSE, Danielle VAN DE DONK
(72' Kirsten VAN DE VEN), Desiree VAN LUNTEREN (13' Dominique JANSSEN), Lieke
MARTENS, Manon MELIS, Vivianne MIEDEMA. (Coach: Roger REIJNERS).
Canada: Erin McLEOD, Carmelina MOSCATO, Josee BELANGER *(YC72)*, Allysha
CHAPMAN, Kadiesha BUCHANAN, Sophie SCHMIDT (81' Rhian WILKINSON), Kaylyn
KYLE (61' Melissa TANCREDI), Ashley LAWRENCE, Jessie FLEMING (61' Desiree
SCOTT), Christine SINCLAIR, Adriana LEON. (Coach: John HERDMAN).
Goals: 10' Ashley LAWRENCE 0-1, 87' Kirsten VAN DE VEN 1-1.
Referee: OK Ri-Hyang (Korea DPR)   Attendance: 45.420

15.06.2015   Investors Group Field, Winnipeg: China PR – New Zealand 2-2 (1-1)
China PR: WANG Fei, LI Dongna, WU Haiyan, LIU Shanshan *(YC75)*, WANG Shanshan,
TANG Jiali (72' WANG Shuang *(YC86)*), HAN Peng (84' LOU Jiahui), REN Guixin, TAN
Ruyin, WANG Lisi (90+3' LI Ying), ZHAO Rong. (Coach: HAO Wei).
New Zealand: Erin NAYLER, Ria PERCIVAL, Abby ERCEG *(YC83)*, Alexandra RILEY,
Rebekah STOTT, Katie DUNCAN *(YC86)*, Annalie LONGO, Betsy HASSETT (46' Katie
BOWEN), Amber HEARN, Hannah WILKINSON, Sarah GREGORIUS (46' Rosie WHITE,
89' Kirsty YALLOP). (Coach: Tony READINGS).
Goals: 28' Rebekah STOTT 0-1, 41' WANG Lisi 1-1 (p), 60' WANG Shanshan 2-1,
64' Hannah WILKINSON 2-2.
Referee: Katalin KULCSAR (Hungary)   Attendance: 26.191

Team	Pld	W	D	L	GF	GA	GD	Pts
Canada	*3*	*1*	*2*	*0*	*2*	*1*	*1*	*5*
China PR	*3*	*1*	*1*	*1*	*3*	*3*	*0*	*4*
Netherlands	*3*	*1*	*1*	*1*	*2*	*2*	*0*	*4*
New Zealand	3	0	2	1	2	3	-1	2

GROUP B

07.06.2015 TD Place Stadiu, Ottawa: Norway – Thailand 4-0 (3-0)
Norway: Ingrid HJELMSETH, Nora Holstad BERGE (46' Marita Skammelsrud LUND), Trine
RØNNING (63' Elise THORSNES), Maren MJELDE, Ingrid Moe WOLD, Lene
MYKJÅLAND, Gry Tofte IMS, Solveig GULBRANDSEN (69' Emilie HAAVI), Kristine
MINDE, Isabell HERLOVSEN, Ada Stolsmo HEGERBERG. (Coach: Even Jostein
PELLERUD).
Thailand: Warapom BOONSING, Sunisa SRANGTHAISONG, Duangnapa SRITALA
(YC74), Natthakam CHINWONG, Warunee PHETWISET (YC51), Pikul KHUEANPET,
Naphat SEESRAUM (59' Orathai SRIMANEE), Anootsara MAIJAREM (90' Thanatta
CHAWONG), Kanjana SUNGNGOEN, Silawan INTAMEE, Rattikan THONGSOMBUT.
(Coach: Nuengrutai SRATHONGVIAN).
Goals: 15' Trine RØNNING 1-0, 29', 34' Isabell HERLOVSEN 2-0, 3-0,
68' Ada Stolsmo HEGERBERG 4-0.
Referee: Anna-Marie KEIGHLEY (New Zealand) Attendance: 20.953

Maren MJELDE missed a penalty kick (75').

07.06.2015 TD Place Stadiu, Ottawa: Germany – Côte d'Ivoire 10-0 (5-0)
Germany: Nadine ANGERER, Saskia BARTUSIAK, Annike KRAHN, Tabea KEMME,
Leonie MAIER, Simone LAUDEHR (73' Lena PETERMANN), Lena GÖßLING, Melanie
LEUPOLZ (17' Melanie BEHRINGER), Anja MITTAG, Célia SASIC (46' Sara DÄBRITZ),
Alexandra POPP. (Coach: Silva NEID).
Côte d'Ivoire: Dominique THIAMALE (YC40), Fatou COULIBALY (YC70), Nina KPAHO
(38' Fernande TCHETCHE), Sophie AGUIE (YC58), Raymonde KACOU, Ida Rebecca
GUEHAI, Rita AKAFFOU (YC36), Binta DIAKITÉ, Josee NAHI (YC86), Nadege ESSOH
(51' Ines NREHY), Rebecca ELLOH (YC66) (72' Ange N'GUESSAN). (Coach: Clementine
TOURE).
Goals: 3', 14' Célia SASIC 1-0, 2-0, 29' Anja MITTAG 3-0, 31' Célia SASIC 4-0,
35', 64' Anja MITTAG 5-0, 6-0, 71' Simone LAUDEHR 7-0, 75' Sara DÄBRITZ 8-0,
79' Melanie BEHRINGER 9-0, 85' Alexandra POPP 10-0.
Referee: Carol Anne CHENARD (Canada) Attendance: 20.953

11.06.2015 TD Place Stadiu, Ottawa: Germany – Norway 1-1 (1-0)
Germany: Nadine ANGERER, Saskia BARTUSIAK (YC59), Annike KRAHN, Tabea
KEMME, Leonie MAIER, Simone LAUDEHR (66' Lena LOTZEN), Lena GÖßLING,
Dzsenifer MAROZSAN, Anja MITTAG (80' Pauline BREMER), Célia SASIC, Alexandra
POPP (70' Sara DÄBRITZ). (Coach: Silva NEID).
Norway: Ingrid HJELMSETH, Marita Skammelsrud LUND, Maren MJELDE, Ingrid Moe
WOLD, Maria THORISDOTTIR, Lene MYKJÅLAND, Gry Tofte IMS (46' Solveig
GULBRANDSEN), Ingrid SCHJELDERUP, Kristine MINDE (60' Elise THORSNES), Isabell
HERLOVSEN (90+1' Emilie HAAVI), Ada Stolsmo HEGERBERG. (Coach: Even Jostein
PELLERUD).
Goals: 6' Anja MITTAG 1-0, 61' Maren MJELDE 1-1.
Referee: Teodora ALBON (Romania) Attendance: 18.987

11.06.2015 TD Place Stadiu, Ottawa: Côte d'Ivoire – Thailand 2-3 (1-2)
Côte d'Ivoire: Dominique THIAMALE, Fatou COULIBALY, Djelika COULIBALY,
Fernande TCHETCHE, Raymonde KACOU, Ida Rebecca GUEHAI (81' Jessica ABY
(YC90+4)), Rita AKAFFOU (46' Rebecca ELLOH), Christine LOHOUES, Binta DIAKITÉ
(34' Josee NAHI), Ines NREHY, Ange N'GUESSAN. (Coach: Clementine TOURE).
Thailand: Warapom BOONSING, Sunisa SRANGTHAISONG, Duangnapa SRITALA,
Natthakam CHINWONG (90+7' Darut CHANGPLOOK), Warunee PHETWISET, Pikul
KHUEANPET, Anootsara MAIJAREM, Kanjana SUNGNGOEN, Silawan INTAMEE, Nisa
ROMYEN (43' Rattikan THONGSOMBUT), Orathai SRIMANEE (73' Thanatta
CHAWONG). (Coach: Nuengrutai SRATHONGVIAN).
Goals: 4' Ange N'GUESSAN 1-0, 26', 45+3' Orathai SRIMANEE 1-1, 1-2,
75' Thanatta CHAWONG 1-3, 88' Josee NAHI 2-3.
Referee: Margaret DOMKA (United States) Attendance: 18.987

15.06.2015 Investors Group Field, Winnipeg: Thailand – Germany 0-4 (0-1)
Thailand: Warapom BOONSING, Sunisa SRANGTHAISONG, Duangnapa SRITALA,
Natthakam CHINWONG, Warunee PHETWISET, Pikul KHUEANPET, Anootsara
MAIJAREM *(YC82)* (87' Alisa RUKPINIJ), Kanjana SUNGNGOEN, Silawan INTAMEE,
Rattikan THONGSOMBUT (89' Darut CHANGPLOOK), Orathai SRIMANEE (79'
Wilaiporn BOOTHDUANG). (Coach: Nuengrutai SRATHONGVIAN).
Germany: Nadine ANGERER, Babett PETER, Annike KRAHN (61' Josephine HENNING),
Melanie BEHRINGER, Bianca SCHMIDT, Dzsenifer MAROZSAN (46' Lena
PETERMANN), Jennifer CRAMER, Melanie LEUPOLZ, Sara DÄBRITZ, Célia SASIC (46'
Anja MITTAG), Lena LOTZEN. (Coach: Silva NEID).
Goals: 24' Melanie LEUPOLZ 0-1, 56', 58' Lena PETERMANN 0-2, 0-3,
73' Sara DÄBRITZ 0-4.
Referee: Gladys LENGWE (Zambia) Attendance: 26.191

15.06.2015 Moncton Stadium, Moncton: Côte d'Ivoire – Norway 1-3 (0-1)
Côte d'Ivoire: Cynthia DJOHORE, Fatou COULIBALY *(YC25)*, Djelika COULIBALY,
Fernande TCHETCHE, Ida Rebecca GUEHAI, Christine LOHOUES (90+4' Rita AKAFFOU),
Josee NAHI, Ines NREHY, Ange N'GUESSAN, Rebecca ELLOH, Nadège CISSÉ (68' Binta
DIAKITÉ, 90+3' Nadege ESSOH). (Coach: Clementine TOURE).
Norway: Ingrid HJELMSETH (80' Silje VESTERBEKKMO), Marita Skammelsrud LUND,
Maria THORISDOTTIR, Lene MYKJÅLAND, Solveig GULBRANDSEN, Ingrid
SCHJELDERUP, Kristine MINDE (46' Ingrid Moe WOLD), Elise THORSNES, Emilie
HAAVI *(YC52)*, Lisa-Marie UTLAND (64' Maren MJELDE), Ada Stolsmo HEGERBERG.
(Coach: Even Jostein PELLERUD).
Goals: 6', 62' Ada Stolsmo HEGERBERG 0-1, 0-2, 67' Solveig GULBRANDSEN 0-3,
71' Ange N'GUESSAN 1-3.
Referee: Jessica Salome DI IORIO (Argentina) Attendance: 7.147

Team	Pld	W	D	L	GF	GA	GD	Pts
Germany	*3*	*2*	*1*	*0*	*15*	*1*	*14*	*7*
Norway	*3*	*2*	*1*	*0*	*8*	*2*	*6*	*7*
Thailand	3	1	0	2	3	10	-7	3
Côte d'Ivoire	3	0	0	3	3	16	-13	0

GROUP C

08.06.2015 BC Place Stadium, Vancouver: Cameroon – Ecuador 6-0 (3-0)
Cameroon: Annette NGO, Yvonne LEUKO, Christine MANIE, Claudine Falonne
MEFFOMETOU Tcheno, Cathy Bou NDJOUH, Raissa FEUDJIO Tchuanyo, Geneviève NGO
MBELECK (61' Francine ZOUGA), Madeleine NGONO (74' Najara CHOUT), Gabrielle
ONGUENE (83' Henriette AKABA), Gaelle ENGANAMOUIT, Jeannette YANGO *(YC38)*.
(Coach: Carl ENOW NGACHU).
Ecuador: Shirley Viviana BERRUZ Aguilar, Nancy Lorena AGUILAR Murillo, Angie Paola
PONCE Baque, Ligia Elena MOREIRA Burgos *(RC66)*, Mayra Fabiola OLVERA Reyes,
Madelin Stefania RIERA Bajana, Kerlly Lizeth REAL Carranza *(YC43)*, Mabel VELARDE
Coba (45' Ingrid Roxana RODRIGUEZ Alvarado *(YC45+2)*), Ambar Gillians TORRES Laz
(54' Giannina Maria LATTANZIO Flores), Monica Rebeca QUINTEROS Cabeza (72'
Katherine Solange ORTIZ Simisterra *(YC70)*), Denise Andrea PESANTES Tenorio. (Coach:
Vanessa ARAUZ).
Goals: 34' Madeleine NGONO 1-0, 36' Gaelle ENGANAMOUIT 2-0,
44' Christine MANIE 3-0 (p), 73' Gaelle ENGANAMOUIT 4-0,
79' Gabrielle ONGUENE 5-0 (p), 90+4' Gaelle ENGANAMOUIT 6-0 (p).
Referee: Katalin KULCSAR (Hungary) Attendance: 25.942

Sent-off: 66' Ligia Elena MOREIRA Burgos.

08.06.2015 BC Place Stadium, Vancouver: Japan – Switzerland 1-0 (1-0)
Japan: Erina YAMANE, Azusa IWASHIMIZU, Saki KUMAGAI, Saori ARIYOSHI, Homare
SAWA (57' Yuri KAWAMURA), Aya MIYAMA, Mizuho SAKAGUCHI, Rumi UTSUGI,
Kozue ANDO (32' Yuika SUGASAWA), Yuki NAGASATO, Shinobu OHNO (90' Nahomi
KAWASUMI). (Coach: Norio SASAKI).
Switzerland: Gaëlle THALMANN *(YC28)*, Ana-Maria CRNOGORCEVIC, Rachel RINAST,
Caroline ABBÉ *(YC90+3)*, Noelle MARITZ, Martina MOSER (81' Cinzia ZEHNDER), Lara
DICKENMANN, Vanessa BERNAUER, Fabienne HUMM (46' Eseosa AIGBOGUN), Lia
WÄLTI, Ramona BACHMANN *(YC22)*. (Coach: Martina VOSS-TECKLENBURG).
Goal: 29' Aya MIYAMA 1-0 (p).
Referee: Lucila VENEGAS Montes (Mexico) Attendance: 25.942

12.06.2015   BC Place Stadium, Vancouver: Switzerland – Ecuador 10-1 (2-0)
Switzerland: Gaëlle THALMANN, Ana-Maria CRNOGORCEVIC, Rachel RINAST, Caroline ABBÉ (51' Cinzia ZEHNDER), Rahel KIWIC (72' Selina KUSTER), Noelle MARITZ (57' Nicole REMUND), Martina MOSER, Fabienne HUMM, Lia WÄLTI, Ramona BACHMANN, Eseosa AIGBOGUN. (Coach: Martina VOSS-TECKLENBURG).
Ecuador: Shirley Viviana BERRUZ Aguilar, Katherine Solange ORTIZ Simisterra (46' Alexandra Lucia Jean SALVADOR Duthie), Nancy Lorena AGUILAR Murillo, Angie Paola PONCE Baque, Ingrid Roxana RODRIGUEZ Alvarado, Mayra Fabiola OLVERA Reyes, Ana Valeria PALACIOS Mendoza (69' Adriana Margarita BARRE Cusme), Kerlly Lizeth REAL Carranza, Mabel VELARDE Coba (79' Erika Paola VASQUEZ Valencia), Monica Rebeca QUINTEROS Cabeza, Denise Andrea PESANTES Tenorio (YC72). (Coach: Vanessa ARAUZ).
Goals: 24' Angie Paola PONCE Baque 1-0 (og), 45+2' Eseosa AIGBOGUN 2-0, 47', 49', 52' Fabienne HUMM 3-0, 4-0, 5-0, 60', 61' Ramona BACHMANN 6-0 (p), 7-0, 64' Angie Paola PONCE Baque 7-1 (p), 71' Angie Paola PONCE Baque 8-1 (og), 76' Martina MOSER 9-1, 81' Ramona BACHMANN 10-1.
Referee: Rita Binti GANI (Malaysia)   Attendance: 31.441

12.06.2015   BC Place Stadium, Vancouver: Japan – Cameroon 2-1 (2-0)
Japan: Ayumi KAIHORI, Yukari KINGA, Azusa IWASHIMIZU, Aya SAMESHIMA, Saki KUMAGAI, Aya MIYAMA, Mizuho SAKAGUCHI (64' Homare SAWA), Rumi UTSUGI, Yuki NAGASATO, Nahomi KAWASUMI (55' Shinobu OHNO), Yuika SUGASAWA (85' Megumi KAMIONOBE). (Coach: Norio SASAKI).
Cameroon: Annette NGO, Yvonne LEUKO, Christine MANIE, Claudine Falonne MEFFOMETOU Tcheno, Cathy Bou NDJOUH, Raissa FEUDJIO Tchuanyo, Geneviève NGO MBELECK (YC43) (46' Francine ZOUGA), Madeleine NGONO (62' Ajara NCHOUT), Gabrielle ONGUENE (72' Augustin EJANGUE), Gaelle ENGANAMOUIT, Jeannette YANGO. (Coach: Carl ENOW NGACHU).
Goals: 6' Aya SAMESHIMA 1-0, 17' Yuika SUGASAWA 2-0, 90' Ajara NCHOUT 2-1.
Referee: Pernilla LARSSON (Sweden)   Attendance: 31.441

16.06.2015   Investors Group Field, Winnipeg: Ecuador – Japan 0-1 (0-1)
Ecuador: Shirley Viviana BERRUZ Aguilar, Katherine Solange ORTIZ Simisterra, Nancy Lorena AGUILAR Murillo (YC52), Angie Paola PONCE Baque, Ingrid Roxana RODRIGUEZ Alvarado, Ligia Elena MOREIRA Burgos, Mayra Fabiola OLVERA Reyes, Erika Paola VASQUEZ Valencia (YC39) (90' Madelin Stefania RIERA Bajana), Kerlly Lizeth REAL Carranza, Monica Rebeca QUINTEROS Cabeza (83' Carina Elizabeth CAICEDO Caicedo), Denise Andrea PESANTES Tenorio. (Coach: Vanessa ARAUZ).
Japan: Miho FUKUMOTO, Aya SAMESHIMA, Asuna TANAKA, Saori ARIYOSHI, Yuri KAWAMURA, Kana KITAHARA (46' Megumi KAMIONOBE), Homare SAWA, Aya MIYAMA, Yuki NAGASATO, Shinobu OHNO (YC17) (75' Asano NAGASATO), Yuika SUGASAWA (80' Mana IWABUCHI). (Coach: Norio SASAKI).
Goal: 5' Yuki NAGASATO 0-1.
Referee: Melissa BORJAS (Honduras)   Attendance: 14.522

16.06.2015 Commonwealth Stadium, Edmonton: Switzerland – Cameroon 1-2 (1-0)
Switzerland: Gaëlle THALMANN, Ana-Maria CRNOGORCEVIC, Rachel RINAST, Selina
KUSTER, Rahel KIWIC (65' Vanessa BERNAUER), Noelle MARITZ, Martina MOSER,
Lara DICKENMANN (80' Nicole REMUND), Fabienne HUMM (69' Eseosa AIGBOGUN),
Lia WÄLTI (YC82), Ramona BACHMANN. (Coach: Martina VOSS-TECKLENBURG).
Cameroon: Annette NGO, Marie Aurelle AWONA, Augustin EJANGUE, Christine MANIE,
Claudine Falonne MEFFOMETOU Tcheno (YC68), Raissa FEUDJIO Tchuanyo (YC19), Ajara
NCHOUT (YC35) (57' Madeleine NGONO), Francine ZOUGA (87' Agathe NGANI),
Gabrielle ONGUENE (90+2' Henriette AKABA), Gaelle ENGANAMOUIT (YC90+2),
Jeannette YANGO. (Coach: Carl ENOW NGACHU).
Goals: 24' Ana-Maria CRNOGORCEVIC 1-0, 47' Gabrielle ONGUENE 1-1,
62' Madeleine NGONO 1-2.
Referee: Claudia Inés UMPIÉRREZ Rodríguez (Uruguay) Attendance: 10.177

Team	Pld	W	D	L	GF	GA	GD	Pts
Japan	3	3	0	0	4	1	3	9
Cameroon	3	2	0	1	9	3	6	6
Switzerland	3	1	0	2	11	4	7	3
Ecuador	3	0	0	3	1	17	-16	0

GROUP D

08.06.2015 Investors Group Field, Winnipeg: Sweden – Nigeria 3-3 (2-0)
Sweden: Rut Hedvig LINDAHL, Emma Sofia BERGLUND (73' Amanda ILESTADT), Nilla
FISCHER, Lina Therese NILSSON, Lisa Karolina Viktoria DAHLKVIST (57' Linda Brigitta
SEMBRANT), Sara Caroline SEGER, Kerstin Ingrid Therese SJÖGRAN, Elin Ingrid Johanna
RUBENSSON, Kosovare ASLLANI (46' Olivia Alma Charlotta SCHOUGH), Eva Sofia
JAKOBSSON, Lotta Eva SCHELIN. (Coach: Pia Mariane SUNDHAGE).
Nigeria: Predious Uzoaru DEDE, Onome EBI, Ngozi EBERE, Osinachi Marvis OHALE,
Josephine Chiwendu CHUKWUNONYE, Ngozi Sonia OKOBI, Halimatu Ibrahim AYINDE,
Evelyn Chiedu NWABUOKU, Ugochi Desire OPARANOZIE, Francisca ORDEGA, Asisat
Lamina OSHOALA. (Coach: Edwin OKON).
Goals: 20' Ugochi Desire OPARANOZIE 1-0 (og), 31' Nilla FISCHER 2-0,
50' Ngozi Sonia OKOBI 2-1, 53' Asisat Lamina OSHOALA 2-2,
60' Linda Brigitta SEMBRANT 3-2, 87' Francisca ORDEGA 3-3.
Referee: OK Ri-Hyang (Korea DPR) Attendance: 31.148

81

08.06.2015 Investors Group Field, Winnipeg: United States – Australia 3-1 (1-1)
United States: Hope Amelia SOLO, Alexandra Blaire (Ali) KRIEGER, Becky
SAUERBRUNN, Meghan KLINGENBERG, Julie ERTZ, Carli LLOYD, Abby WAMBACH,
Lauren HOLIDAY *(YC56)*, Megan RAPINOE *(YC64)* (87' Morgan BRIAN), Sydney
LEROUX (79' Alexandra (Alex) MORGAN), Christen PRESS (68' Tobin HEATH). (Coach:
Jillian ELLIS).
Australia: Melissa BARBIERI HUDSON, Emily VAN EGMOND, Laura ALLEWAY (83'
Ashleigh SYKES), Steph CATLEY, Servet UZUNLAR, Elise KELLOND, Katrina GORRY
(80' Alanna KENNEDY), Lisa DE VANNA, Samantha KERR, Michelle HEYMAN (69'
Kyah SIMON), Caitlin FOORD. (Coach: Alen STAJCIC).
Goals: 12' Megan RAPINOE 1-0, 27' Lisa DE VANNA 1-1, 61' Christen PRESS 2-1,
78' Megan RAPINOE 3-1.
Referee: Claudia Inés UMPIÉRREZ Rodríguez (Uruguay) Attendance: 31.148

12.06.2015 Investors Group Field, Winnipeg: Australia – Nigeria 2-0 (1-0)
Australia: Lydia WILLIAMS, Emily VAN EGMOND, Laura ALLEWAY, Steph CATLEY,
Alanna KENNEDY, Elise KELLOND, Katrina GORRY (62' Tameka BUTT), Lisa DE
VANNA, Samantha KERR, Kyah SIMON (87' Michelle HEYMAN), Caitlin FOORD.
(Coach: Alen STAJCIC).
Nigeria: Predious Uzoaru DEDE, Onome EBI, Ngozi EBERE, Osinachi Marvis OHALE (52'
Ugo NJOKU), Josephine Chiwendu CHUKWUNONYE *(YC60)*, Ngozi Sonia OKOBI,
Halimatu Ibrahim AYINDE, Evelyn Chiedu NWABUOKU *(YC42)*, Ugochi Desire
OPARANOZIE (54' Perpetua Ijeoma NKWOCHA), Francisca ORDEGA, Asisat Lamina
OSHOALA (84' Courtney Ozioma DIKE). (Coach: Edwin OKON).
Goals: 29', 68' Kyah SIMON 1-0, 2-0.
Referee: Stéphanie FRAPPART (France) Attendance: 32.716

12.06.2015 Investors Group Field, Winnipeg: United States – Sweden 0-0
United States: Hope Amelia SOLO, Alexandra Blaire (Ali) KRIEGER, Becky
SAUERBRUNN, Meghan KLINGENBERG, Julie ERTZ, Morgan BRIAN (58' Amy
RODRIGUEZ), Carli LLOYD, Lauren HOLIDAY, Megan RAPINOE, Sydney LEROUX (78'
Alexandra (Alex) MORGAN), Christen PRESS (67' Abby WAMBACH). (Coach: Jillian
ELLIS).
Sweden: Rut Hedvig LINDAHL, Nilla FISCHER, Lina Therese NILSSON (70' Linda Brigitta
SEMBRANT), Amanda ILESTADT, Jessica Marie SAMUELSSON, Lisa Karolina Viktoria
DAHLKVIST, Sara Caroline SEGER, Kerstin Ingrid Therese SJÖGRAN (75' Emilia
APPELQVIST), Elin Ingrid Johanna RUBENSSON, Eva Sofia JAKOBSSON, Lotta Eva
SCHELIN. (Coach: Pia Mariane SUNDHAGE).
Referee: Sachiko YAMAGISHI (Japan) Attendance: 32.716

16.06.2015 Commonwealth Stadium, Edmonton: Australia – Sweden 1-1 (1-1)
Australia: Lydia WILLIAMS, Emily VAN EGMOND, Laura ALLEWAY, Steph CATLEY, Alanna KENNEDY, Elise KELLOND, Katrina GORRY (85' Tameka BUTT), Lisa DE VANNA (63' Larissa CRUMMER), Samantha KERR, Kyah SIMON (72' Michelle HEYMAN), Caitlin FOORD. (Coach: Alen STAJCIC).
Sweden: Rut Hedvig LINDAHL, Nilla FISCHER, Lina Therese NILSSON (74' Kosovare ASLLANI), Amanda ILESTADT, Jessica Marie SAMUELSSON, Lisa Karolina Viktoria DAHLKVIST, Sara Caroline SEGER, Kerstin Ingrid Therese SJÖGRAN, Elin Ingrid Johanna RUBENSSON (76' Sara Kristina THUNEBRO), Eva Sofia JAKOBSSON, Lotta Eva SCHELIN. (Coach: Pia Mariane SUNDHAGE).
Goals: 5' Lisa DE VANNA 1-0, 15' Eva Sofia JAKOBSSON 1-1
Referee: Lucila VENEGAS Montes (Mexico) Attendance: 10.177

16.06.2015 BC Place Stadium, Vancouver: Nigeria – United States 0-1 (0-1)
Nigeria: Predious Uzoaru DEDE, Onome EBI *(YC43)*, Ngozi EBERE, Sarah Ihechiluru Amaka NNODIM *(YC38,YC69)*, Josephine Chiwendu CHUKWUNONYE *(YC59)*, Ngozi Sonia OKOBI *(YC68)*, Chiedu NWABUOKU, Ukpong Esther SUNDAY (50' Halimatu Ibrahim AYINDE), Francisca ORDEGA (77' Cecilia Ngibo NKU), Asisat Lamina OSHOALA, Courtney Ozioma DIKE (50' Ugochi Desire OPARANOZIE). (Coach: Edwin OKON).
United States: Hope Amelia SOLO, Alexandra Blaire (Ali) KRIEGER, Becky SAUERBRUNN, Meghan KLINGENBERG, Julie ERTZ, Tobin HEATH (80' Christie PEARCE), Carli LLOYD, Abby WAMBACH, Lauren HOLIDAY, Megan RAPINOE (74' Shannon BOXX), Alexandra (Alex) MORGAN (66' Sydney LEROUX). (Coach: Jillian ELLIS).
Goal: 45' Abby WAMBACH 0-1.
Referee: Kateryna MONZUL (Ukraine) Attendance: 52.193

Sent-off: 69' Sarah Ihechiluru Amaka NNODIM.

Team	Pld	W	D	L	GF	GA	GD	Pts
United States	*3*	*2*	*1*	*0*	*4*	*1*	*3*	*7*
Australia	*3*	*1*	*1*	*1*	*4*	*4*	*0*	*4*
Sweden	*3*	*0*	*3*	*0*	*4*	*4*	*0*	*3*
Nigeria	3	0	1	2	3	6	-3	1

GROUP E

09.06.2015   Stade Olympique, Montréal: Spain – Costa Rica 1-1 (1-1)
Spain: AINHOA TIRAPU de Goñi, MARTA TORREJÓN Moya, LEIRE LANDA Iroz,
IRENE PAREDES Hernandez, CELIA JIMÉNEZ Delgado *(YC44)* (63' RUTH GARCÍA
García), María VICTORIA LOSADA Gómez, ALÈXIA PUTELLAS Segura, SONIA
BERMÚDEZ Tribano (72' MARTA CORREDERA Rueda), VERÓNICA (Vero) BOQUETE
Giadans, NATALIA Teresa de PABLOS Sanchón, JENIFER HERMOSO Fuentes (84'
PRISCILA BORJA Moreno). (Coach: IGNACIO QUEREDA Laviña).
Costa Rica: Dinnia Cecilia DIAZ Artavia, Carol SANCHEZ Cruz, Lixy RODRIGUEZ
Zamora, Diana Carolina SAENZ Brown, Shirley CRUZ Traña, Katherine Maria ALVARADO
Aguilar, Raquel (Rocky) RODRÍGUEZ Cedeño, Carolina Paola VENEGAS Morales (80'
Cristin Yorleny GRANADOS Gomez), Wendy Patricia Salas ACOSTA, Maria Fernanda
BARRANTES Rojas (74' Karla Gabriela VILLALOBOS Duran), Melissa HERRERA Monge
(88' Gabriela GUILLEN Alvarez). (Coach: Amelia VALVERDE Villalobos).
Goals: 13' María VICTORIA LOSADA Gómez 1-0, 14' Raquel (Rocky) RODRÍGUEZ
Cedeño 1-1.
Referee: Jessica Salome DI IORIO (Argentina)   Attendance: 10.175

09.06.2015   Stade Olympique, Montréal: Brazil – Korea Republic 2-0 (1-0)
Brazil: LUCIANA Maria Dionizio, MÔNICA Hickmann Alves, FABIANA da Silva Simões,
RAFAELLE Leone Carvalho Souza (82' GESSICA do Nascimento), TAMIRES Cassia Dias
Gomes, Miraildes Maciel Mota "FORMIGA", ANDRESSA Cavalari Machry (81' RAQUEL
Fernandes dos Santos), MARTA Vieira da Silva, CRISTIANE Rozeira de Souza Silva,
ANDRESSA ALVES da Silva (90+1' Rafaela de Miranda Travalao "RAFINHA"), Thaysa de
Moraes Rosa Moreno "ISA". (Coach: Oswaldo Fumeiro Alvarez "VADÃO").
Korea Republic: KIM Jung-Mi, LEE Eun-Mi, KIM Do-Yeon, KIM Hye-Ri, SIM Seo-Yeon,
JEON Ga-Eul, JI So-Yeon, KWON Hah-Nul (77' LEE So-Dam), CHO So-Hyun *(YC53)*,
KANG Yu-Mi (90+1' PARK Hee-Young), YOO Young-A (67' JUNG Seol-Bin). (Coach:
YOON Deuk-Yeo).
Goals: 33' Miraildes Maciel Mota "FORMIGA" 1-0, 53' MARTA Vieira da Silva 2-0 (p).
Referee: Esther STAUBLI (Switzerland)   Attendance: 10.175

13.06.2015 Stade Olympique, Montréal: Brazil – Spain 1-0 (1-0)
Brazil: LUCIANA Maria Dionizio, MÔNICA Hickmann Alves, FABIANA da Silva Simões
(77' POLIANA Barbosa Medeiros), RAFAELLE Leone Carvalho Souza, TAMIRES Cassia
Dias Gomes, Mirailes Maciel Mota "FORMIGA", ANDRESSA Cavalari Machry, MARTA
Vieira da Silva, CRISTIANE Rozeira de Souza Silva (89' RAQUEL Fernandes dos Santos
(YC90+3)), ANDRESSA ALVES da Silva, Thaysa de Moraes Rosa Moreno "ISA" (60'
DARLENE de Souza Reguera). (Coach: Oswaldo Fumeiro Alvarez "VADÃO").
Spain: AINHOA TIRAPU de Goñi, MARTA TORREJÓN Moya, LEIRE LANDA Iroz
(YC23), IRENE PAREDES Hernandez, CELIA JIMÉNEZ Delgado, María VICTORIA
LOSADA Gómez, ALÈXIA PUTELLAS Segura, VIRGINIA TORRECILLA Reyes (77'
SONIA BERMÚDEZ Tribano), VERÓNICA (Vero) BOQUETE Giadans, NATALIA Teresa
de PABLOS Sanchón (71' Silvia Meseguer Bellido "MESI"), MARTA CORREDERA Rueda
(70' PRISCILA BORJA Moreno). (Coach: IGNACIO QUEREDA Laviña).
Goal: 44' ANDRESSA ALVES da Silva 1-0.
Referee: Carol Anne CHENARD (Canada)   Attendance: 28.623

13.06.2015 Stade Olympique, Montréal: Korea Republic – Costa Rica 2-2 (2-1)
Korea Republic: KIM Jung-Mi, LEE Eun-Mi, KIM Hye-Ri (YC70) (84' LIM Seon-Joo),
HWANG Bo-Ram (YC86), SIM Seo-Yeon, JEON Ga-Eul, JI So-Yeon, KWON Hah-Nul, CHO
So-Hyun, KANG Yu-Mi (63' JUNG Seol-Bin), YOO Young-A (77' LEE Geum-Min (YC81)).
(Coach: YOON Deuk-Yeo).
Costa Rica: Dinnia Cecilia DIAZ Artavia, Carol SANCHEZ Cruz, Lixy RODRIGUEZ
Zamora, Diana Carolina SAENZ Brown, Shirley CRUZ Traña, Katherine Maria ALVARADO
Aguilar, Raquel (Rocky) RODRÍGUEZ Cedeño, Cristin Yorleny GRANADOS Gomez,
Wendy Patricia Salas ACOSTA, Maria Fernanda BARRANTES Rojas (76' Karla Gabriela
VILLALOBOS Duran), Melissa HERRERA Monge. (Coach: Amelia VALVERDE
Villalobos).
Goals: 17' Melissa HERRERA Monge 0-1, 21' JI So-Yeon 1-1 (p), 25' JEON Ga-Eul 2-1,
89' Karla Gabriela VILLALOBOS Duran 2-2.
Referee: Carina Susanna VITULANO (Italy)   Attendance: 28.623

17.06.2015 Moncton Stadium, Moncton: Costa Rica – Brazil 0-1 (0-0)
Costa Rica: Dinnia Cecilia DIAZ Artavia, Carol SANCHEZ Cruz, Lixy RODRIGUEZ
Zamora, Diana Carolina SAENZ Brown, Shirley CRUZ Traña, Katherine Maria ALVARADO
Aguilar (86' Fabiola Maria SANCHEZ Jimenez), Raquel (Rocky) RODRÍGUEZ Cedeño,
Cristin Yorleny GRANADOS Gomez (57' Carolina Paola VENEGAS Morales), Wendy
Patricia Salas ACOSTA, Maria Fernanda BARRANTES Rojas (72' Karla Gabriela
VILLALOBOS Duran), Melissa HERRERA Monge. (Coach: Amelia VALVERDE
Villalobos).
Brazil: LUCIANA Maria Dionizio, MÔNICA Hickmann Alves (66' GESSICA do
Nascimento), RAFAELLE Leone Carvalho Souza, POLIANA Barbosa Medeiros, TAMIRES
Cassia Dias Gomes, ROSANA dos Santos Augusto, MAURINE Dornelles Gonçalves,
ANDRESSA Cavalari Machry, DARLENE de Souza Reguera (59' BEATRIZ Zaneratto João),
GABRIELA Maria Zanotti Demoner (78' Rafaela de Miranda Travalao "RAFINHA"),
RAQUEL Fernandes dos Santos. (Coach: Oswaldo Fumeiro Alvarez "VADÃO").
Goal: 83' RAQUEL Fernandes dos Santos 0-1.
Referee: Thalia MITSI (Greece) Attendance: 9.543

17.06.2015 TD Place Stadium, Ottawa: Korea Republic – Spain 2-1 (0-1)
Korea Republic: KIM Jung-Mi, LEE Eun-Mi, KIM Hye-Ri (46' KIM Soo-Yun), HWANG Bo-
Ram (YC69), SIM Seo-Yeon, JEON Ga-Eul, JI So-Yeon, KWON Hah-Nul, CHO So-Hyun,
KANG Yu-Mi (77' PARK Hee-Young), PARK Eun-Sun (59' YOO Young-A). (Coach:
YOON Deuk-Yeo).
Spain: AINHOA TIRAPU de Goñi, MARTA TORREJÓN Moya, LEIRE LANDA Iroz,
IRENE PAREDES Hernandez, CELIA JIMÉNEZ Delgado, María VICTORIA LOSADA
Gómez (57' Silvia Meseguer Bellido "MESI"), ALÈXIA PUTELLAS Segura, VIRGINIA
TORRECILLA Reyes (YC57), VERÓNICA (Vero) BOQUETE Giadans, NATALIA Teresa de
PABLOS Sanchón (64' SONIA BERMÚDEZ Tribano), MARTA CORREDERA Rueda (75'
ERIKA VÁZQUEZ Morales). (Coach: IGNACIO QUEREDA Laviña).
Goals: 29' VERÓNICA (Vero) BOQUETE Giadans 0-1, 53' CHO So-Hyun 1-1,
78' KIM Soo-Yun 2-1.
Referee: Anna-Marie KEIGHLEY (New Zealand) Attendance: 21.562

Team	Pld	W	D	L	GF	GA	GD	Pts
Brazil	3	3	0	0	4	0	4	9
Korea Republic	3	1	1	1	4	5	-1	4
Costa Rica	3	0	2	1	3	4	-1	2
Spain	3	0	1	2	2	4	-2	1

GROUP F

09.06.2015 Moncton Stadium, Moncton: France – England 1-0 (1-0)
France: Sarah BOUHADDI, Laura GEORGES, Wendie RENARD, Jessica HOUARA, Laure
BOULLEAU, Camille ABILY, Amandine HENRY, Louisa NECIB (87' Claire LAVOGEZ),
Elodie THOMIS (71' Kenza DALI), Eugénie LE SOMMER (81' Elise BUSSAGLIA),
Gaëtane THINEY. (Coaches: Corinne DIACRE & Philippe BERGEROO).
England: Karen BARDSLEY, Alexandra SCOTT (68' Francesca KIRBY), Stephanie
HOUGHTON, Laura BASSETT, Claire RAFFERTY, Lucy BRONZE, Katie CHAPMAN
(YC66) (76' Jade MOORE), Fara WILLIAMS, Jill SCOTT, Eniola ALUKO, Ellen WHITE
(60' Toni DUGGAN). (Coach: Mark SAMPSON).
Goal: 29' Eugénie LE SOMMER 1-0.
Referee: Thalia MITSI (Greece)   Attendance: 11.686

09.06.2015 Moncton Stadium, Moncton: Colombia – Mexico 1-1 (0-1)
Colombia: Derly Stefany CASTAÑO Cardozo, Carolina ARIAS Vidal, Katherine Nataly
ARIAS Peña, Angela Corina CLAVIJO Silva, Natalia GAITÁN Laguado (YC25), Daniele
MONTOYA Quiróz (YC55), Hazleydi Yoreli RINCÓN Torres, Lady Patricia ANDRADE
Rodríguez (77' Tatiana ARIZA Díaz), Diana Carolina OSPINA García (87' Yisela CUESTA
Bejarano), Maria Catalina USME Pineda (78' Ingrid Yulieth VIDAL Isaza), Oriánica
VELÁSQUEZ Herrera (YC34). (Coach: Fabián Felipe TABORDA).
Mexico: Cecilia SANTIAGO Cisneros (YC18), Alina Lisi GARCIAMENDEZ Rowold,
Valeria Aurora MIRANDA Rodriguez, Christina MURILLO Ruiz, Kenti ROBLES Salas,
Nayeli RANGEL Hernandez, Sandra Stephany MAYOR Gutierrez, Veronica Raquel PEREZ
Murillo, Verónica Charlyn CORRAL Ang, Renae Nicole CUÉLLAR Cuéllar (79' Jennifer
Marie RUIZ Brown), Mónica OCAMPO Medina (87' Claudia Fabiola IBARRA Muro).
(Coach: Leonardo CUÉLLAR Rivera).
Goals: 35' Veronica Raquel PEREZ Murillo 0-1, 82' Daniele MONTOYA Quiróz 1-1.
Referee: Therese Raissa NEGUEL (Cameroon)   Attendance: 11.686

13.06.2015 Moncton Stadium, Moncton: France – Colombia 0-2 (0-1)
France: Sarah BOUHADDI, Laura GEORGES, Wendie RENARD, Jessica HOUARA, Laure
BOULLEAU, Camille ABILY, Louisa NECIB (63' Claire LAVOGEZ), Elise BUSSAGLIA
(63' Amandine HENRY), Kenza DALI (77' Marie Laure DELIE), Eugénie LE SOMMER,
Gaëtane THINEY. (Coaches: Corinne DIACRE & Philippe BERGEROO).
Colombia: Sandra Milena SEPÚLVEDA Lopera (YC69), Carolina ARIAS Vidal, Katherine
Nataly ARIAS Peña, Angela Corina CLAVIJO Silva, Natalia GAITÁN Laguado, Daniele
MONTOYA Quiróz, Hazleydi Yoreli RINCÓN Torres (87' Isabella ECHEVERRI Restrepo),
Lady Patricia ANDRADE Rodríguez (90+2' Tatiana ARIZA Díaz), Diana Carolina OSPINA
García (YC79), Oriánica VELÁSQUEZ Herrera, Ingrid Yulieth VIDAL Isaza (55' Maria
Catalina USME Pineda). (Coach: Fabián Felipe TABORDA).
Goals: 19' Lady Patricia ANDRADE Rodríguez 0-1, 90+3' Maria Catalina USME Pineda 0-2.
Referee: QIN Liang (China PR)   Attendance: 13.138

13.06.2015 Moncton Stadium, Moncton: England – Mexico 2-1 (0-0)
England: Karen BARDSLEY, Stephanie HOUGHTON, Laura BASSETT, Claire RAFFERTY
(53' Alex GREENWOOD), Lucy BRONZE (85' Alexandra SCOTT), Fara WILLIAMS, Jill
SCOTT (66' Karen CARNEY *(YC90+2)*), Jade MOORE, Eniola ALUKO, Toni DUGGAN,
Francesca KIRBY. (Coach: Mark SAMPSON).
Mexico: Cecilia SANTIAGO Cisneros, Alina Lisi GARCIAMENDEZ Rowold *(YC64)*, Bianca
Elissa SIERRA Garcia (46' Valeria Aurora MIRANDA Rodriguez), Kenti ROBLES Salas,
Nayeli RANGEL Hernandez, Sandra Stephany MAYOR Gutierrez, Veronica Raquel PEREZ
Murillo, Jennifer Marie RUIZ Brown, Verónica Charlyn CORRAL Ang, Renae Nicole
CUÉLLAR Cuéllar (77' Maria Guadalupe SANCHEZ Morales), Mónica OCAMPO Medina
(89' Claudia Fabiola IBARRA Muro). (Coach: Leonardo CUÉLLAR Rivera).
Goals: 70' Francesca KIRBY 1-0, 82' Karen CARNEY 2-0,
90+1' Claudia Fabiola IBARRA Muro 2-1.
Referee: Anna-Marie KEIGHLEY (New Zealand) Attendance: 13.138

17.06.2015 TD Place Stadium, Ottawa: Mexico – France 0-5 (0-4)
Mexico: Cecilia SANTIAGO Cisneros, Alina Lisi GARCIAMENDEZ Rowold, Valeria Aurora
MIRANDA Rodriguez *(YC62)*, Kenti ROBLES Salas, Greta Alejandra ESPINOZA Casas,
Nayeli RANGEL Hernandez (83' Christina MURILLO Ruiz), Sandra Stephany MAYOR
Gutierrez (46' Arianna Jeanette ROMERO Tellez), Veronica Raquel PEREZ Murillo *(YC87)*,
Jennifer Marie RUIZ Brown, Verónica Charlyn CORRAL Ang (46' Renae Nicole CUÉLLAR
Cuéllar), Mónica OCAMPO Medina. (Coach: Leonardo CUÉLLAR Rivera).
France: Sarah BOUHADDI, Laura GEORGES, Wendie RENARD, Jessica HOUARA, Laure
BOULLEAU (78' Sabrina DELANNOY), Camille ABILY 70' Elise BUSSAGLIA),
Amandine HENRY, Amel MAJRI, Elodie THOMIS, Eugénie LE SOMMER (63' Gaëtane
THINEY), Marie Laure DELIE. (Coaches: Corinne DIACRE & Philippe BERGEROO).
Goals: 1' Marie Laure DELIE 0-1, 9' Jennifer Marie RUIZ Brown 0-2 (og),
13', 36' Eugénie LE SOMMER 0-3, 0-4, 80' Amandine HENRY 0-5.
Referee: Sachiko YAMAGISHI (Japan) Attendance: 21.562

17.06.2015 Stade Olympique, Montréal: England – Colombia 2-1 (2-0)
England: Karen BARDSLEY, Alexandra SCOTT *(YC65)*, Casey STONEY, Stephanie
HOUGHTON, Alex GREENWOOD, Fara WILLIAMS, Jade MOORE, Jordan NOBBS, Karen
CARNEY (56' Lianne SANDERSON), Toni DUGGAN (81' Jodie TAYLOR), Francesca
KIRBY (66' Josanne POTTER). (Coach: Mark SAMPSON).
Colombia: Sandra Milena SEPÚLVEDA Lopera *(YC85)*, Carolina ARIAS Vidal *(YC37)*,
Katherine Nataly ARIAS Peña, Angela Corina CLAVIJO Silva, Natalia GAITÁN Laguado,
Daniele MONTOYA Quiróz, Hazleydi Yoreli RINCÓN Torres (74' Tatiana ARIZA Díaz),
Lady Patricia ANDRADE Rodríguez, Diana Carolina OSPINA García (83' Leicy Maria
SANTOS Herrera), Maria Catalina USME Pineda *(YC36)* (58' Ingrid Yulieth VIDAL Isaza),
Oriánica VELÁSQUEZ Herrera. (Coach: Fabián Felipe TABORDA).
Goals: 15' Karen CARNEY 1-0, 38' Fara WILLIAMS 2-0 (p),
90+4' Lady Patricia ANDRADE Rodríguez 2-1.
Referee: Carol Anne CHENARD (Canada) Attendance: 13.862

Team	Pld	W	D	L	GF	GA	GD	Pts
France	*3*	*2*	*0*	*1*	*6*	*2*	*4*	*6*
England	*3*	*2*	*0*	*1*	*4*	*3*	*1*	*6*
Colombia	3	1	1	1	4	3	1	4
Mexico	3	0	1	2	2	8	-6	1

ROUND OF 16

20.06.2015 TD Place Stadium, Ottawa: Germany – Sweden 4-1 (2-0)
Germany: Nadine ANGERER, Saskia BARTUSIAK *(YC28)*, Annike KRAHN, Tabea
KEMME (77' Jennifer CRAMER), Leonie MAIER, Simone LAUDEHR, Lena GÖßLING,
Melanie LEUPOLZ (46' Dzsenifer MAROZSAN), Anja MITTAG, Célia SASIC, Alexandra
POPP (89' Lena LOTZEN). (Coach: Silva NEID).
Sweden: Rut Hedvig LINDAHL, Emma Sofia BERGLUND (80' Jenny Josefina
HJOHLMAN), Linda Brigitta SEMBRANT, Nilla FISCHER, Amanda ILESTADT *(YC35)*,
Jessica Marie SAMUELSSON (46' Lina Therese NILSSON), Sara Caroline SEGER, Kerstin
Ingrid Therese SJÖGRAN, Elin Ingrid Johanna RUBENSSON (67' Kosovare ASLLANI), Eva
Sofia JAKOBSSON, Lotta Eva SCHELIN (YC68). (Coach: Pia Mariane SUNDHAGE).
Goals: 24' Anja MITTAG 1-0, 35', 78' Célia SASIC 2-0 (p), 3-0,
82' Linda Brigitta SEMBRANT 3-1, 88' Dzsenifer MAROZSAN 4-1.
Referee: OK Ri-Hyang (Korea DPR) Attendance: 22.486

20.06.2015 Commonwealth Stadium, Edmonton: China PR – Cameroon 1-0 (1-0)
China PR: WANG Fei, LI Dongna, WU Haiyan, LIU Shanshan, WANG Shanshan (90+1' GU
Yasha), TANG Jiali (40' WANG Shuang), HAN Peng, REN Guixin, TAN Ruyin, WANG Lisi
(72' LOU Jiahui), ZHAO Rong. (Coach: HAO Wei).
Cameroon: Annette NGO, Yvonne LEUKO, Marie Aurelle AWONA, Christine MANIE,
Claudine Falonne MEFFOMETOU Tcheno *(YC90+3)*, Raissa FEUDJIO Tchuanyo, Madeleine
NGONO (74' Henriette AKABA), Francine ZOUGA (64' Ajara NCHOUT), Gabrielle
ONGUENE, Gaelle ENGANAMOUIT, Jeannette YANGO. (Coach: Carl ENOW NGACHU).
Goal: 12' WANG Shanshan 1-0.
Referee: Bibiana STEINHAUS (Germany) Attendance: 15.958

21.06.2015 Moncton Stadium, Moncton: Brazil – Australia 0-1 (0-0)
Brazil: LUCIANA Maria Dionizio, MÔNICA Hickmann Alves, FABIANA da Silva Simões
(YC14), RAFAELLE Leone Carvalho Souza, TAMIRES Cassia Dias Gomes (83' RAQUEL
Fernandes dos Santos), Miraildes Maciel Mota "FORMIGA", ANDRESSA Cavalari Machry,
MARTA Vieira da Silva *(YC81)*, CRISTIANE Rozeira de Souza Silva, ANDRESSA ALVES
da Silva, Thaysa de Moraes Rosa Moreno "ISA" (83' BEATRIZ Zaneratto João). (Coach:
Oswaldo Fumeiro Alvarez "VADÃO").
Australia: Lydia WILLIAMS, Emily VAN EGMOND, Laura ALLEWAY, Steph CATLEY,
Alanna KENNEDY, Elise KELLOND, Tameka BUTT (72' Katrina GORRY), Lisa DE
VANNA, Samantha KERR, Michelle HEYMAN (64' Kyah SIMON), Caitlin FOORD.
(Coach: Alen STAJCIC).
Goal: 80' Kyah SIMON 0-1.
Referee: Teodora ALBON (Romania)   Attendance: 12.054

21.06.2015 Stade Olympique, Montréal: France – Korea Republic 3-0 (2-0)
France: Sarah BOUHADDI, Laura GEORGES, Wendie RENARD, Jessica HOUARA, Laure
BOULLEAU, Camille ABILY (77' Kheira HAMRAOUI *(YC80)*), Amandine HENRY, Louisa
NECIB, Elodie THOMIS, Eugénie LE SOMMER (74' Gaëtane THINEY), Marie Laure
DELIE (84' Kadidiatou DIANI). (Coaches: Corinne DIACRE & Philippe BERGEROO).
Korea Republic: KIM Jung-Mi, LEE Eun-Mi *(YC33)*, KIM Do-Yeon, KIM Soo-Yun, SIM
Seo-Yeon, JEON Ga-Eul, KWON Hah-Nul (60' LEE So-Dam), CHO So-Hyun, KANG Yu-Mi
(78' PARK Hee-Young), LEE Geum-Min *(YC85)*, PARK Eun-Sun (55' YOO Young-A).
(Coach: YOON Deuk-Yeo).
Goals: 4' Marie Laure DELIE 1-0, 8' Elodie THOMIS 2-0, 47' Marie Laure DELIE 3-0.
Referee: Jessica Salome DI IORIO (Argentina)   Attendance: 15.518

21.06.2015 BC Place Stadium, Vancouver: Canada – Switzerland 1-0 (0-0)
Canada: Erin McLEOD, Rhian WILKINSON (88' Marie Eve NAULT), Lauren
SESSELMANN, Ashley LAWRENCE (76' Kaylyn KYLE), Josee BELANGER, Allysha
CHAPMAN, Kadiesha BUCHANAN *(YC74)*, Sophie SCHMIDT, Desiree SCOTT, Christine
SINCLAIR *(YC14)*, Melissa TANCREDI (69' Jonelle FILIGNO). (Coach: John HERDMAN).
Switzerland: Gaëlle THALMANN, Ana-Maria CRNOGORCEVIC, Rachel RINAST (80'
Rahel KIWIC), Selina KUSTER *(YC46)* (61' Vanessa BÜRKI), Caroline ABBÉ, Noelle
MARITZ, Martina MOSER (72' Fabienne HUMM), Lara DICKENMANN, Vanessa
BERNAUER, Lia WÄLTI, Ramona BACHMANN. (Coach: Martina VOSS-
TECKLENBURG).
Goal: 52' Josee BELANGER 1-0.
Referee: Anna-Marie KEIGHLEY (New Zealand)   Attendance: 53.855

22.06.2015   TD Place Stadium, Ottawa: Norway – England 1-2 (0-0)
Norway: Ingrid HJELMSETH, Trine RØNNING (46' Maria THORISDOTTIR), Marita
Skammelsrud LUND, Maren MJELDE, Ingrid Moe WOLD (87' Lisa-Marie UTLAND), Lene
MYKJÅLAND, Gry Tofte IMS, Solveig GULBRANDSEN, Kristine MINDE (70' Elise
THORSNES), Isabell HERLOVSEN, Ada Stolsmo HEGERBERG. (Coach: Even Jostein
PELLERUD).
England: Karen BARDSLEY, Stephanie HOUGHTON, Laura BASSETT, Claire RAFFERTY,
Lucy BRONZE, Katie CHAPMAN, Fara WILLIAMS, Jade MOORE, Karen CARNEY, Toni
DUGGAN (63' Jodie TAYLOR), Francesca KIRBY (54' Jill SCOTT). (Coach: Mark
SAMPSON).
Goals: 54' Solveig GULBRANDSEN 1-0, 61' Stephanie HOUGHTON 1-1,
76' Lucy BRONZE 1-2.
Referee: Esther STAUBLI (Switzerland)   Attendance: 19.829

22.06.2015   Commonwealth Stadium, Edmonton: United States – Colombia 2-0 (0-0)
United States: Hope Amelia SOLO, Alexandra Blaire (Ali) KRIEGER (81' Lori
CHALUPNY), Becky SAUERBRUNN, Meghan KLINGENBERG, Julie ERTZ, Tobin
HEATH, Carli LLOYD, Abby WAMBACH (69' Morgan BRIAN), Lauren HOLIDAY
(YC17), Megan RAPINOE *(YC41)* (75' Christen PRESS), Alexandra (Alex) MORGAN.
(Coach: Jillian ELLIS).
Colombia: Catalina PÉREZ Jaramillo *(RC47)*, Carolina ARIAS Vidal, Katherine Nataly
ARIAS Peña, Angela Corina CLAVIJO Silva *(YC65)*, Natalia GAITÁN Laguado, Daniele
MONTOYA Quiróz (85' Leicy Maria SANTOS Herrera), Hazleydi Yoreli RINCÓN Torres
(72' Maria Catalina USME Pineda), Lady Patricia ANDRADE Rodríguez, Diana Carolina
OSPINA García, Oriánica VELÁSQUEZ Herrera, Ingrid Yulieth VIDAL Isaza (49' Derly
Stefany CASTAÑO Cardozo). (Coach: Fabián Felipe TABORDA).
Goals: 53' Alexandra (Alex) MORGAN 1-0, 66' Carli LLOYD 2-0 (p).
Referee: Stéphanie FRAPPART (France)   Attendance: 19.412

Abby WAMBACH missed a penalty kick (49').

Sent-off: 47' Catalina PÉREZ Jaramillo.

23.06.2015   BC Place Stadium, Vancouver: Japan – Netherlands 2-1 (1-0)
Japan: Ayumi KAIHORI, Azusa IWASHIMIZU, Aya SAMESHIMA, Saori ARIYOSHI
(YC51), Aya MIYAMA, Mizuho SAKAGUCHI, Rumi UTSUGI, Saki KUMAGAI, Yuki
NAGASATO, Shinobu OHNO (86' Mana IWABUCHI), Nahomi KAWASUMI (80' Homare
SAWA). (Coach: Norio SASAKI).
Netherlands: Loes GEURTS, Mandy VAN DEN BERG, Stephanie VAN DER GRAGT, Merel
VAN DONGEN (86' Tessel MIDDAG), Anouk DEKKER, Sherida SPITSE, Danielle VAN
DE DONK (53' Kirsten VAN DE VEN), Desiree VAN LUNTEREN, Lieke MARTENS,
Manon MELIS, Vivianne MIEDEMA. (Coach: Roger REIJNERS).
Goals: 10' Saori ARIYOSHI 1-0, 78' Mizuho SAKAGUCHI 2-0,
90+2' Kirsten VAN DE VEN 2-1.
Referee: Lucila VENEGAS Montes (Mexico)   Attendance: 28.717

QUARTER-FINALS

26.06.2015 Stade Olympique, Montréal: Germany – France 1-1 (0-0, 1-1)
Germany: Nadine ANGERER, Babett PETER, Annike KRAHN, Tabea KEMME, Leonie
MAIER, Simone LAUDEHR, Lena GÖßLING *(YC68)* (79' Melanie BEHRINGER), Melanie
LEUPOLZ *(YC91)*, Anja MITTAG *(YC37)* (46' Dzsenifer MAROZSAN *(YC68)*), Célia
SASIC, Alexandra POPP (70' Sara DÄBRITZ). (Coach: Silva NEID).
France: Sarah BOUHADDI, Laura GEORGES *(YC57)*, Wendie RENARD, Jessica HOUARA,
Camille ABILY, Amandine HENRY, Louisa NECIB, Amel MAJRI, Elodie THOMIS (69'
Claire LAVOGEZ), Eugénie LE SOMMER (90' Gaëtane THINEY), Marie Laure DELIE
(YC55) (101' Kheira HAMRAOUI). (Coaches: Corinne DIACRE & Philippe BERGEROO).
Goals: 64' Louisa NECIB 0-1, 84' Célia SASIC 1-1 (p).
Referee: Carol Anne CHENARD (Canada) Attendance: 24.859

*Penalties: Melanie BEHRINGER 1-0, Gaëtane THINEY 1-1, Simone LAUDEHR 2-1,
Camille ABILY 2-2, Babett PETER 3-2, Louisa NECIB 3-3, Dzsenifer
MAROZSAN 4-3, Wendie RENARD 4-4, Célia SASIC 5-4, Claire
LAVOGEZ missed.*

After extra time, Germany won 5-4 on penalties.

26.06.2015 TD Place Stadium, Ottawa: China PR – United States 0-1 (0-0)
China PR: WANG Fei, LI Dongna, WU Haiyan *(YC50)*, LIU Shanshan, WANG Shanshan,
HAN Peng (75' TANG Jiali), REN Guixin, TAN Ruyin (58' PANG Fengyue), WANG Lisi,
LOU Jiahui (35' WANG Shuang), ZHAO Rong. (Coach: HAO Wei).
United States: Hope Amelia SOLO, Alexandra Blaire (Ali) KRIEGER, Becky
SAUERBRUNN, Meghan KLINGENBERG, Julie ERTZ, Tobin HEATH, Morgan BRIAN,
Carli LLOYD, Kelley O'HARA (61' Christen PRESS), Alexandra (Alex) MORGAN (81'
Heather O'REILLY), Amy RODRIGUEZ (86' Abby WAMBACH). (Coach: Jillian ELLIS).
Goal: 51' Carli LLOYD 0-1.
Referee: Carina Susanna VITULANO (Italy) Attendance: 24.141

27.06.2015 Commonwealth Stadium, Edmonton: Australia – Japan 0-1 (0-0)
Australia: Lydia WILLIAMS, Emily VAN EGMOND, Laura ALLEWAY, Steph CATLEY,
Alanna KENNEDY, Elise KELLOND, Katrina GORRY (76' Michelle HEYMAN), Lisa DE
VANNA (67' Larissa CRUMMER), Samantha KERR, Kyah SIMON (89' Ashleigh SYKES),
Caitlin FOORD. (Coach: Alen STAJCIC).
Japan: Ayumi KAIHORI, Azusa IWASHIMIZU *(YC27)*, Aya SAMESHIMA, Saori
ARIYOSHI, Aya MIYAMA, Mizuho SAKAGUCHI (90' Homare SAWA), Rumi UTSUGI,
Saki KUMAGAI, Yuki NAGASATO, Shinobu OHNO (72' Mana IWABUCHI), Nahomi
KAWASUMI. (Coach: Norio SASAKI).
Goal: 87' Mana IWABUCHI 0-1.
Referee: Kateryna MONZUL (Ukraine) Attendance: 19.814

27.06.2015 BC Place Stadium, Vancouver: England – Canada 2-1 (2-1)
England: Karen BARDSLEY (52' Siobhan CHAMBERLAIN), Stephanie HOUGHTON,
Laura BASSETT, Claire RAFFERTY, Lucy BRONZE, Katie CHAPMAN, Fara WILLIAMS
(79' Ellen WHITE), Jill SCOTT, Jade MOORE *(YC63)*, Karen CARNEY (90+3' Casey
STONEY), Jodie TAYLOR. (Coach: Mark SAMPSON).
Canada: Erin McLEOD, Rhian WILKINSON (62' Diana MATHESON), Lauren
SESSELMANN *(YC90+3)*, Ashley LAWRENCE, Josee BELANGER, Allysha CHAPMAN,
Kadiesha BUCHANAN, Sophie SCHMIDT, Desiree SCOTT (77' Kaylyn KYLE), Christine
SINCLAIR, Melissa TANCREDI (71' Adriana LEON). (Coach: John HERDMAN).
Goals: 11' Jodie TAYLOR 1-0, 14' Lucy BRONZE 2-0, 42' Christine SINCLAIR 2-1.
Referee: Claudia Inés UMPIÉRREZ Rodríguez (Uruguay)   Attendance: 54.027

SEMI-FINALS

30.06.2015 Stade Olympique, Montréal: United States – Germany 2-0 (0-0)
United States: Hope Amelia SOLO, Alexandra Blaire (Ali) KRIEGER, Becky
SAUERBRUNN *(YC38)*, Meghan KLINGENBERG, Julie ERTZ *(YC59)*, Tobin HEATH (75'
Kelley O'HARA), Morgan BRIAN, Carli LLOYD, Lauren HOLIDAY, Megan RAPINOE (80'
Abby WAMBACH), Alexandra (Alex) MORGAN (90+3' Sydney LEROUX). (Coach: Jillian
ELLIS).
Germany: Nadine ANGERER, Saskia BARTUSIAK, Annike KRAHN *(YC67)*, Tabea
KEMME, Leonie MAIER *(YC34)*, Simone LAUDEHR, Lena GÖßLING, Melanie LEUPOLZ,
Anja MITTAG (78' Dzsenifer MAROZSAN), Célia SASIC, Alexandra POPP. (Coach: Silva
NEID).
Goals: 69' Carli LLOYD 1-0 (p), 84' Kelley O'HARA 2-0.
Referee: Teodora ALBON (Romania)   Attendance: 51.176

Célia SASIC missed a penalty kick (60').

01.07.2015 Commonwealth Stadium, Edmonton: Japan – England 2-1 (1-1)
Japan: Ayumi KAIHORI, Azusa IWASHIMIZU, Aya SAMESHIMA, Saori ARIYOSHI, Aya
MIYAMA, Mizuho SAKAGUCHI, Rumi UTSUGI, Saki KUMAGAI, Yuki NAGASATO
(YC90), Shinobu OHNO (70' Mana IWABUCHI), Nahomi KAWASUMI. (Coach: Norio
SASAKI).
England: Karen BARDSLEY, Stephanie HOUGHTON, Laura BASSETT, Claire RAFFERTY
(YC31), Lucy BRONZE (75' Alexandra SCOTT), Katie CHAPMAN, Fara WILLIAMS (85'
Karen CARNEY), Jill SCOTT, Jade MOORE, Toni DUGGAN, Jodie TAYLOR (60' Ellen
WHITE). (Coach: Mark SAMPSON).
Goals: 32' Aya MIYAMA 1-0 (p), 40' Fara WILLIAMS 1-1 (p),
90+2' Laura BASSETT 2-1 (og).
Referee: Anna-Marie KEIGHLEY (New Zealand)   Attendance: 31.467

THIRD PLACE MATCH

04.07.2015 Commonwealth Stadium, Edmonton: Germany – England 0-1 (0-0, 0-0)
Germany: Nadine ANGERER, Saskia BARTUSIAK, Babett PETER, Tabea KEMME,
Melanie BEHRINGER (46' Melanie LEUPOLZ), Simone LAUDEHR, Lena GÖßLING (101'
Alexandra POPP), Bianca SCHMIDT, Sara DÄBRITZ, Célia SASIC (73' Anja MITTAG),
Lena PETERMANN. (Coach: Silva NEID).
England: Karen BARDSLEY *(YC83)*, Stephanie HOUGHTON, Laura BASSETT *(YC92)*,
Lucy BRONZE, Alex GREENWOOD, Katie CHAPMAN *(YC77)* (80' Lianne
SANDERSON), Fara WILLIAMS (112' Casey STONEY), Jill SCOTT, Josanne POTTER,
Karen CARNEY, Ellen WHITE (61' Eniola ALUKO). (Coach: Mark SAMPSON).
Goal: 108' Fara WILLIAMS 0-1.
Referee: OK Ri-Hyang (Korea DPR) Attendance: 21.483

FINAL

05.07.2015 BC Place Stadium, Vancouver: United States – Japan 5-2 (4-1)
United States: Hope Amelia SOLO, Alexandra Blaire (Ali) KRIEGER, Becky
SAUERBRUNN, Meghan KLINGENBERG, Julie ERTZ, Tobin HEATH (79' Abby
WAMBACH), Morgan BRIAN, Carli LLOYD, Lauren HOLIDAY, Megan RAPINOE (61'
Kelley O'HARA), Alexandra (Alex) MORGAN (86' Christie PEARCE). (Coach: Jillian
ELLIS).
Japan: Ayumi KAIHORI, Azusa IWASHIMIZU (33' Homare SAWA *(YC82)*), Aya
SAMESHIMA, Saori ARIYOSHI, Aya MIYAMA, Mizuho SAKAGUCHI, Rumi UTSUGI,
Saki KUMAGAI, Yuki NAGASATO, Shinobu OHNO (60' Mana IWABUCHI *(YC85)*),
Nahomi KAWASUMI (39' Yuika SUGASAWA). (Coach: Norio SASAKI).
Goals: 3', 5' Carli LLOYD 1-0, 2-0, 14' Lauren HOLIDAY 3-0, 16' Carli LLOYD 4-0,
27' Yuki NAGASATO 4-1, 52' Julie ERTZ 4-2 (og), 54' Tobin HEATH 5-2.
Referee: Kateryna MONZUL (Ukraine) Attendance: 53.341

The United States won the World Cup.